GW01003176

# THE OUTLINED BIBLE

## ROBERT LEE

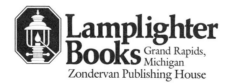

Lamplighter Books Grand Rapids, Michigan
Zondervan Publishing House

THE OUTLINED BIBLE
Copyright © 1981 by Pickering & Inglis Ltd.
Glasgow, Scotland

Zondervan edition published in 1982 by special arrangement with Pickering & Inglis

Lamplighter Books are published by Zondervan
Publishing House, 1415 Lake Drive, S.E.,
Grand Rapids, Michigan 49506

**Library of Congress Cataloging in Publication Data**

Lee, Robert, 1872–1956.
    The outlined Bible.

    Originally published: Glasgow: Pickering & Inglis, [192-?]
    1. Bibles—Outlines, syllabi, etc.   I. Title.
BS591.L43   1982        220'.02'02        82-2559
ISBN 0-310-44821-2        AACR2

First revised edition    1982

*Printed in the United States of America*

91  92  93  94  95 / CH / 13  12  11  10  9

# PREFACE

The following Bible Studies, which have been designed and arranged to show at a glance the contents of each separate book of the Bible, formed part of a five years' course at the Mildmay Bible School, which I had the honour to conduct. The majority of them were planned and prepared with no idea whatever of publication, and they have been published only at the urgent request of many Missionaries and Christian workers who listened to them, and of friends in many parts who have been helped by them.

As a preparation for a more exhaustive study of the Word, this system is indispensable. In order to read the 66 books of the Bible with some degree of intelligence, it is necessary to understand something of their human authors, the various purposes they had in mind when writing them, their distinctive styles, and other peculiarities.

I need hardly say that these studies are by no means exhaustive. The limited space at my disposal only permitted the barest of comments, and the rather large and unwieldy appearance is essential in order that each book may be seen at a glance. I ought also to say that, to be of the fullest service, these studies must be used as originally intended. Each one present at the School received a copy of the Analysis; during the Lecture they had it before them with the opened Bible; after the Lecture they took it home with them, and went carefully over the Bible book with its aid.

ROBERT LEE

# PREFACE TO NEW EDITION

"Through many years Robert Lee's OUTLINED BIBLE has sufficiently proved its value to generations of Bible-lovers. The need to reset the type gave opportunity to lay out the pages more in accord with modern taste and techniques, but very little else has been changed. The occasionally necessary abbreviation has not lost or altered anything of Robert Lee's thought. Even the temptation to refer to more modern translations of the scriptures has been resisted, out of respect for Lee's immense knowledge of the English Authorised Version (AV/KJV). But Lee wished also to introduce the (English) Revised Version of 1881 (RV) to wider circles of Bible readers, and doubtless today would have referred also to more modern versions. To quote from even a selection of these would seriously overload the notes: the reader will be able, and at many points he will be encouraged, to make his own comparisons with the translation he prefers.

With its old message in new dress, THE OUTLINED BIBLE is sent out yet again with the prayer that it may introduce still further generations of students to the priceless treasures of the Word of God.

# ANALYSES of the BOOKS of the OLD TESTAMENT

| Book | Key Word or Phrase | Theme |
|---|---|---|
| GENESIS | BEGINNING | The failure of man met by the salvation of God |
| EXODUS | REDEEM | Redemption by blood |
| LEVITICUS | HOLINESS, ATONEMENT | Access to God through blood: Holiness imperative |
| NUMBERS | SERVICE, SOJOURNING, WORK, WAR | The redeemed saved to serve: beware of unbelief |
| DEUTERONOMY | OBEDIENCE | The motive and necessity of obedience |
| JOSHUA | POSSESS | The faithfulness of God declared and demonstrated |
| JUDGES | 'RIGHT IN HIS OWN EYES' | Spiritual declension and God's grace in restoration |
| RUTH | REST, REDEEM | Rest through redemption and union |
| 1 SAMUEL | PRAYED | The place and power of prayer in life |
| 2 SAMUEL | 'BEFORE THE LORD' | Be sure your sin will find you out |
| 1 KINGS | 'AS DAVID HIS FATHER' | Jehovah, the sovereign ruler of Israel |
| 2 KINGS | 'ACCORDING TO THE WORD OF THE LORD' | The fulfilment of the word of the Lord |
| 1 CHRONICLES | 'THOU REIGNEST OVER ALL' | Jehovah as Sovereign Lord |
| 2 CHRONICLES | 'PREPARETH HIS HEART TO SEEK GOD' | Seeking and serving the Lord |
| EZRA | THE WORD OF THE LORD | The place and power of the word of God in the life of his people |
| NEHEMIAH | PRAYER, WORK | The conditions of successful work for God |
| ESTHER | 'FOR SUCH A TIME AS THIS' | The reality of the divine providence |
| JOB | TRIAL | Trials and Suffering for our education |
| PSALMS | WORSHIP | 'Worship the Lord in the beauty of holiness' |
| PROVERBS | WORDS TO RULE LIFE | Godliness is intensely practical |
| ECCLESIASTES | 'UNDER THE SUN' | Life without God is a disappointment |
| SONG OF SOLOMON | LOVE | The Communion of Christ with his people |
| ISAIAH | SALVATION | National salvation through judgment and grace |
| JEREMIAH | BACKSLIDING, RETURN, AMEND, LOVED | God's certain judgment: God's eternal love |
| LAMENTATIONS | 'IS IT NOTHING TO YOU?' | The misery of sin: The compassion of Jehovah |
| EZEKIEL | THE GLORY OF THE LORD | The goodness and severity of God |
| DANIEL | 'THE MOST HIGH RULETH' | The universal sovereignty of God |
| HOSEA | RETURN | God's method in restoring backsliders |
| JOEL | 'THE DAY OF THE LORD' | The value and importance of repentance |
| AMOS | PUNISHMENT | National sin means national judgment |
| OBADIAH | RETRIBUTION | The perils of pride and anti-semitism |
| JONAH | 'FOR I KNEW' | God, the God of the Gentiles |
| MICAH | 'WHO IS A GOD LIKE UNTO THEE?' | God's Hatred of injustice and ritualism |
| NAHUM | 'UTTER END' | The awful doom of the apostate |
| HABAKKUK | WHY? | God's consistency in view of permitted evil |
| ZEPHANIAH | JEALOUSY | God — a jealous God |
| HAGGAI | 'THE WORD OF THE LORD' | God first in life and service |
| ZECHARIAH | 'I AM JEALOUS' | God's care for his people |
| MALACHI | 'YE SAY' | Remember, repent, return, rehearse |

# 1
# The Book of Genesis

**Key word: Beginning**
**Key verse: 1: 1**
**Theme: The failure of man under every condition met by the salvation of God**

### Hatred of enemy of mankind

There are two books in the Bible the great enemy of mankind especially hates, and has bent all his energies to discredit, and they are Genesis and Revelation. He has attempted to overthrow Genesis by attacks of scientists and other critics, and Revelation by persuading men it is too mysterious. Why this dislike? Because they both prophesy his downfall — Genesis tells us who would bring this about, and Revelation gives details of its execution.

### Its great value

1 In many respects it is the most important book in the Bible. Every great leading fact, truth and revelation is found here in germ — as the oak in the acorn. Melanchthon stated: 'The whole book of Genesis excels in sweetness all other books and histories,' and 'There is no more beautiful and lovable little book.'
2 Dr Bullinger says: 'Genesis is the seed-plot of the whole Bible, and it is essential to the true understanding of its every part. It is the foundation on which the divine revelation rests, and on which it is built up. It is not only the foundation of all truth, but it enters into and forms part of all subsequent inspiration; and is at once the warp and woof of Holy Writ.' Genesis is the book of beginnings.

### Its author and origin

1 The book was written by Moses. But how did he get his materials? Is it a mere compilation from ancient documents? If we examine the old relics with this, we see the improbability of that theory.
2 Is it a written record of traditional lore? Many think so, and it is not as impossible as some imagine. Milton, in his 'Paradise Lost', depicts Gabriel relating to Adam the wonders of creation. This is pure fiction; but the Lord, no doubt, would communicate coveted knowledge to Adam, who told Methuselah, who told Noah, who told Shem, who told Abraham, who told Isaac, who told Jacob, who told Joseph, from whose writings Moses would learn it.
3 But Acts 7: 37, 38 leaves us in no doubt as to its origin — it was received by Moses from God — it was born on Mount Sinai.
4 Dr Adam Clark writes: 'The narrative is so simple, so much like truth, so consistent everywhere with itself, so correct in its dates, so impartial in its biography, so accurate in its philosophical details, so pure in its morality, and so benevolent in its design, as amply to demonstrate that it never could have had an earthly origin.'

### Style

It is written in prose, not poetry. This is important. Poetry forms handy clothing for myth and legend, as other ancient books. Thus Genesis is written, not in a mythical, but an historical style — for it is history and fact, not fable.

### Its message

1 Its distinctive message is: The failure of man, under every condition, met by the salvation of God.
2 It was necessary for man to know by failure his own weakness and insufficiency, before he would voluntarily choose God.
3 In this book man is seen to fail: (1) Amidst ideal environment (Eden). (2) Under the rule of conscience (from Fall to Deluge). (3) Under patriarchal rule (from Noah to Joseph). Note, the book begins with God, and ends with a coffin.
4 But human failure is met by the divine grace and activity. Where sin abounded grace did much more abound.

### Analysis

1 It could be divided into eleven sections, the expression 'the generation of' being the beginning of each section except the first — as for instance, Section I, 2: 3. Section II, 2: 4 to 4: 26. Section III, 5: 1 to 6: 8, etc.
2 But for easy analysis, taking 'Beginning' as the key-word, we have nine sections:

## PRIMEVAL HISTORY, covering over 2,000 years

**1 The beginning of the material (1: 1-25)**
1 V.1 gives us the original creation.
2 Isaiah 45: 18 tells us that God did not create as we find it in v.2.
3 Note 2 Peter 3: 5, 6.
4 The six days were days of reconstruction.

**2 Beginning of the human race (1: 26 to 2: 25)**
1 Man created, not evolved.
2 Placed in charge of a reclaimed wilderness, for 'Eden' is Accadian for 'wilderness'.

**3 Beginning of human sin (3: 1-7)**
1 Tampering with word of God. The woman subtracted from and added to the word of the Lord.
2 She 'saw', 'took', 'gave'.

**4 Beginning of revelation of redemption (3: 8-24)**
1 First promise of a redeemer, the beginning of all subsequent revelations.
2 The next time we meet the cherubim we find no sword because of blood (Ex. 25: 20).

**5 Beginnings of human family life (4: 1-15)**
1 First family.
2 First family quarrel, and that over religion.
3 Note RV of v.7, where sin is likened to the crouching of a wild beast.

**6 Beginning of godless civilization (4: 16 to 9: 29)**
1 First city built, and city life originated by a murderer.
2 Note RV of 4: 23 and 26.

**7 Beginning of nations of the world (c. 10)**
1 A very important section.
2 Here we have the title deeds of the nations.

**8 Beginning of confusion of language (c. 11)**
1 A first attempt at unity apart from God.
2 This attempt at Babel to unify mankind will be repeated by Anti-Christ, see Rev. 17.

## PATRIARCHAL HISTORY, covering over 300 years

**Beginning of the Hebrew race (cc. 12 to 50)**
1 This section is largely biographical.
2 We have history of Abraham, Isaac, and Jacob.

# 2
# The Book of Exodus

**Key word: Redeem**
**Key verses: 3:8; 12:23**
**Theme: Redemption by blood**

### Livingstone and Exodus

Livingstone made the Bible his constant study. It appears that in later life the books of Genesis and Exodus were constantly in his mind, Moses being his favourite Bible hero.

### Exodus the sequel to Genesis

Between the close of Genesis and the opening of Exodus 3½ centuries intervene. Between the going down of Jacob to Egypt and the commencement of the persecution, 115 years must have passed. One has said this 'silence of 3½ centuries is almost awful in its grandeur, like the loneliness of Sinai in the mount of the Lord'. Exodus is the sequel to Genesis. Genesis speaks of man's failure under every test, and in every condition; but Exodus shows us God hastening to man's rescue, to man's redemption, coming forth to emancipate and enrich. Its key verses are as above — 3:8 gives God's declaration, and 12:23 shows how it was accomplished. Exodus is the book of redemption. Note how the book opens and closes. It begins in darkness and gloom, yet ends in glory; it commences by telling how God came down in grace to deliver an enslaved people, and ends by declaring how God came down in glory to dwell in the midst of a redeemed people.

### The pattern of our redemption

In the construction of an engine or a ship, a design has to be drawn, and a pattern made. Our salvation was the design of God before the foundation of the world — the pattern we find in the Book of Exodus. 'Exodus is the historical picture of the outworking of divine grace in the redemption and recovery of man by God to himself by Jesus Christ, who is at once our great apostle (Moses) and high priest (Aaron).' 'The story of Exodus is repeated in every soul that seeks deliverance from the enmeshing and enervating influence of the world. From this point of view, the book is human, from the first verse to the last. The things that happened were by way of figure, and they were written for our admonition.' We study Exodus in order to see God's way of delivering sinful man, and his gracious and glorious purposes in thus rescuing him.

### Analysis

The book is in two main divisions, and five sections.

---

## NARRATIVE (cc. 1 to 18)

### Bondage

**(cc. 1, 2)**
1 Here we have the sad condition of the people, whom God eventually redeemed.
2 Events:
Birth of Moses
Adoption of Moses
Renunciation of Moses
Flight of Moses
Marriage of Moses
3 Israel's awful suffering:
Disturbed them
Purified them
Unified them
Disenchanted them

### Redemption

**(3 : 1 to 15: 21)**
1 Here we behold God coming down in grace to deliver Israel, and we see how redemption was accomplished — by blood.
2 Events:
Call of Moses
Moses' return to Egypt
Conflicts with Pharaoh
Israel emancipated
3 Life of Moses summarised:
40 years thought he was somebody.
40 years learning he was a nobody.
40 years discovering what God can do with a nobody.

### Education

**(15: 22 to 18: 27)**
1 Here is begun the spiritual education of Israel; all these events were designed to teach them absolute dependence upon God.
2 Events:
Marah and Elim
Wilderness of Sin
Rephidim
Amalek and Jethro.
3 Note: — Elims generally follow the Marahs; and divine love will sweeten the Marahs it does not remove.

---

## LEGISLATIVE (cc. 19 to 40)

### Consecration

**(cc. 19 to 23)**
1 Here we are taught that the redeemed must do the will of their redeemer, must consecrate themselves to his service. For the redeemed, a divine rule for faith and conduct is provided.
2 Event:
The giving of the moral law.
3 Now he writes his Law upon the fleshy tables of redeemed hearts and gives his Holy Spirit to cause them to walk in his ways.

### Worship

**(cc. 24 to 40)**
1 Redeemed ones must be worshipping ones; and must worship only in God's own appointed way.
2 Event:
The giving of the ceremonial law.
3 A very rich section. God designed *everything* about the Tabernacle; consequently not one sacred article should escape our prayerful study.

# 3
# The Book of Leviticus

**Key words: Holiness, Atonement**
**Key verses: 17: 11; 19: 2**
**Themes: 1 Access of redeemed to God only through blood**
**2 Holiness of the redeemed imperative**

## Title

'Leviticus' — the name commonly given to the third book of Moses — was the title given to it by the 'Seventy' when they translated it from the original Hebrew into Greek. Its Hebrew title is 'Va-yich-rah', i.e., 'And he called.' The former is a man-given name, inferring that it contains ordinances pertaining to the Levites, yet the Levites are only once mentioned incidentally, (25: 32, 33); the latter is the divine name, and is more in keeping with the contents, viz. God's call to the redeemed to access, communion, and worship in his presence, and to holiness of body and soul.

## Time

The whole of the instructions given and the events recorded in this book come between April 1st, when they set up the Tabernacle (Exod. 40: 2, 17, also see Lev. 1: 1), and May 20th, when they departed from Mount Sinai (Numbers 10: 11). 'Considered as embracing the history of one month only,' wrote Dr Parker, 'this may claim to be the most remarkable book in the Old Testament.'

## For whom?

This is a book for redeemed people, showing how God is to be approached and worshipped. In Genesis we see man ruined, in Exodus man redeemed, in Leviticus man worshipping. All its types relate to worship, as those of Exodus relate to redemption. Leviticus is the book of worship.

## Peculiarities

1 Note how majestically the book opens. It is the first of only three that have a like beginning, the other two being Numbers and Joshua. Such an introductory sentence ('and the Lord called') always indicates the communication that follows to be of first importance.
2 A great Bible scholar has pointed out that in Leviticus 'The Holy Spirit is not once named, though referred to in all the other books of the Pentateuch, because all here relates to Christ, and it is the Spirit's work to glorify Christ.'
3 No other book in the Bible contains so many direct messages from Jehovah as this. 'The Lord spake,' 'said,' or 'commanded,' are met with 56 times; 'I am Jehovah' 21 times; 'I am Jehovah, your God' 21 times; 'I am' 3; and 'I, Jehovah, do' twice.

## Message

1 The key-word of the book is 'Holy'. It is met with at least 87 times. Its next basal key-word is 'Atonement', occurring at least 45 times.
2 The problem is, How can a sinful man approach a holy God? How is he to gain access to God? Who is to decide this question? God alone must determine how. This book declares that even his redeemed ones can only gain access to him, with its consequent privilege of communion and worship, on the basis of sacrifice through shedding of blood.
3 It has also another message. One of the surprises of the book is its insistence on the holiness of the body, as well as that of the soul. This book teaches that the redeemed must be holy, because their redeemer is holy (19: 2).

---

## THE HOLINESS OF GOD

---

**1 Chapters 1 to 10 (key 17:11)**
Because of that holiness, the access of the redeemed to Jehovah can only be secured on the basis of sacrifice through blood shedding.
1 THE FIVE OFFERINGS, each of which represents a distinct aspect of the one offering of our Lord Jesus (1: 1 to 6: 7).
2 THE LAW OF THE OFFERINGS, giving particulars as to order, arrangement, etc. (5: 8 to 6: 30).

3 THE PRIESTHOOD:
(cc. 8 to 10)
(a) Call (8:1-5),
(b) Cleansing (v.6),
(c) Clothing (vv.7-13),
(d) Atonement (vv.14-29),
(e) Anointing (v.30),
(f) Food (vv.31-36),
(g) Ministry (c.9),
(h) Failure (c. 10).

**2 Chapters 11 to 27 (key 19: 2)**
Because of that holiness, the holiness of both body and soul of the redeemed is both imperative and compulsory.
1 LAWS OF PURITY (cc. 11 to 16)
Holy people must have
(a) Pure food (c. 11),
(b) Pure bodies (12: 1 to 14: 32),
(c) Pure homes (14: 33-57),
(d) Pure habits (c. 15),
(e) constant resort to the blood (c. 16). (This 16th chapter is the great atonement chapter.)

2 SUNDRY LAWS, in recapitulation, (cc. 17 to 26)
Holy people must have
(a) Pure worship (17: 1-9),
(b) Sacred regard for blood (vv.10-16),
(c) Pure morals (c. 18),
(d) Pure customs, clothing, etc. (cc. 19 to 26).
(Note the feasts in c. 23.)
3 LAWS CONCERNING VOWS (c. 27).

# 4
# The Book of Numbers

**Key words: Service, Sojourning, Work, War**
**Key verses: 14: 8, 9**
**Theme: The redeemed 1 are saved to serve; 2 must beware of unbelief**

## Name

Numbers is the name by which the fourth book of Moses is generally known because it records two numberings of Israel — that at Sinai (c. 1) and the one in Moab (c. 26). But its name in the Hebrew Bible is B'midbar, which means, 'In the wilderness', and this seems the better title, as it covers all the events of the book, viz. all the wanderings and experiences of Israel in the wilderness. It is the book of the wilderness.

## Character

The book is partly historical and partly legislative. It is the book of pilgrimage, of warfare, service, and, alas, of failure.

## Message

This book has a three-fold message: (1) One of its principal thoughts is that of service. This is the message we meet with right on its threshold. The Lord's people are saved to serve. Note how significant is the order of the messages of these first four Bible books: In Genesis we see man ruined, in Exodus man redeemed, in Leviticus man worshipping, and now in Numbers, man in service. This is the divine order. Only a saved and worshipping soul is qualified for service. (2) Its second message is the indispensableness of order in service and walk. Order is heaven's first law. Here we note how well organised the camp and the service of the tabernacle were, and how orderly the Lord desired the daily walk of the Israelites to be. (3) It has a third message: The failure of Israel looms large as we read its pages; and that failure was due to unbelief, therefore this book cries to every redeemed one: *'Beware of unbelief!'* Thank God it was not all failure! In the last section we see Israel victorious owing to their restoration to God's favour.

---

**1 At Sinai (Time, 20 days: See 1: 1, and 10: 11)**
## Orderly Service
**in the wilderness**
**(cc. 1 to 10)**
**The Lord's Service:**
1 In battle (c. 1)
2 In a well ordered camp (c. 2)
3 in the tabernacle (cc. 3, 4)
4 In a pure camp (c. 5)
5 In a Nazarite life (c. 6)
6 In unsolicited gifts (c. 7)
7 In Aaronic and Levitical service (c. 8)
(Note. 'Work' and 'Service' rendered in RV margin as 'Warfare' (4: 3, 23.)
**Other Matters:**
1 Passover legislation (9: 1-14)
2 Guiding cloud (9: 15-23)
3 Trumpet legislation (c. 10)

**2 From Sinai to Kadesh (Time, 37 years, 11 months)**
## Sad Failure
**in the wilderness**
**(cc. 11 to 20, with 21: 5-9; c. 25)**

A very sad section: eight murmurings altogether, as follows:
1 Against the WAY God led them (11: 1-3)
2 The FOOD he fed them with (11: 4-35)
3 Against the LEADER he set over them (c. 12)
4 Against the LAND he promised them (cc. 13, 14)
5 They murmured against God's righteous VERDICT pronounced on them (14: 39-45)
6 And against his APPOINTMENTS (cc. 16, 17)
7 They murmured against THIRST (20: 2-13)

8 And because of God's PROVISION (21: 4-9)
During these 37 years Israel almost ceases to have a history; it is almost a blank. Hence significance of the murmurings of 20: 2-13, the first trial, and failure, of the new generation, showing they were no better than their fathers. Note the legislation of cc. 15, 18, 19.

**3 In Moab (Time, 9 months, 10 days)**
## Glorious Victory
**in the wilderness**
**(21: 1-4, 10 to 36: 13)**
The predominant note of this section is victory, though there are some failures. The old generation had passed away as punishment for their sin at Kadesh. God now takes up Israel again.
1 Victory over King Arad (21: 1-3)
2 Victory over King Sihon and King Og (21: 21-35)
3 Balaam and Balak (cc. 22 to 25)
4 Second census (c. 26), (decrease of 1,820 since the numbering of c. 1)
5 The law of inheritance (c. 27)
6 Joshua to succeed Moses (c. 27)
7 Ordering of the offerings and vows (cc. 28 to 30)
8 Victory over Midian (c. 31)
9 Preparations to enter the land (32: 1 to 36: 13)

# 5
# The Book of Deuteronomy

**Key word: Obedience**
**Key verses: 5: 29; 10: 12, 13; 11: 26-28; 28: 1**
**Theme: The true motive for obedience, and the necessity of obedience**

## The book
Deuteronomy is the fifth and last book of Moses. Its name means 'The Second Law'. Not that it contains new laws, but that the laws given at Sinai 39 years before are here reviewed and commented upon. And there was urgent need of such rehearsal. With two exceptions (Caleb and Joshua) the adults who had left Egypt and received the Law at Sinai had died, and it was therefore necessary that the new generation should have the Law rehearsed and emphasized to them. This Moses did in a series of eight discourses in the plains of Moab at the end of the 40 years' wanderings, and just one month before the nation crossed over the Jordan to take possession of the promised land. The addresses were first delivered orally, and then written (see 1: 3; 31: 24-26).

## Jesus' use of it
One would judge that this book was a special favourite of our adorable Lord in the days of his childhood, youth, and manhood, for it was the only book from which he quoted in his conflict with the Tempter (see Matt. 4: 1-11; Luke 4: 1-13; with Deut. 8: 3; 6: 16; 6: 13; and 10: 20). Judging from the many quotations in their writings, it must also have been the favourite book of the prophets.

## Satan's dread of it
This book has been most fiercely attacked by the 'Higher' critical school. The date of the book of Deuteronomy is a crucial question in the criticism of the Old Testament. The critics declare that the book was not written by Moses, but by some unknown author at least 600 years after; that the Pentateuch was 'in great part composed to glorify the priesthood at Jerusalem, and that the book of Deuteronomy in particular was produced to establish Jerusalem as the central and only acceptable shrine for the worship of Israel'. How comes it then that the name Jerusalem is not only entirely absent from Deuteronomy but also is not once mentioned in any other of the books of Moses? Remembering our Lord's use of Deuteronomy, need we wonder at Satan's hatred of it, and attempts to discredit it?

## Some notable contents
This book contains (1) the first reference to the 'children of Belial' (13: 13); (2) the first time we meet with the death by hanging on a tree (21: 22, 23); (3) the only reference in the Old Testament to that great vision recorded in Exodus c.3, which led to Moses' call and Israel's deliverance (33: 16, 'Him that dwelt in the bush'); and the great prediction about a coming Prophet-Christ (18: 15-19).

## More than a review
But this book is much more than a book of recapitulation and review of the law given at Sinai. It has forcefully been said that 'it reviews the past with an eye to the future'. The whole book is a divine treatise on obedience. Moses already had tangible evidence (see Num. 20: 1-6) that the new generation were no better than their fathers, and he knew that everything depended upon their obedience — life itself, possession of Canaan, victory over foes, prosperity, happiness. So with all the force of his own ardent nature the leader pleads with the new generation. He pointed out that God longed for their obedience (5: 29) because they were his own (1: 3; 14: 1), because he loved them (4: 37; 7: 7, 8), and desired to preserve and prosper them (4: 1, 40; 5: 29; 6: 2, 3, 24, etc.); and that out of gratitude to God for his amazing grace, mercy and privilege, they should render such obedience (4: 7, 8; 5: 6; 4: 33, etc.). The full force and beauty of this book can only be discovered by reading it at one sitting. It is a heart-stirring, heart-moving appeal!

## Analysis
There are eight separate and distinct discourses, with a final chapter on the death of Moses.

---

**First Discourse**
### Retrospect
**(1:1 to 4:43)**
1 Failure at Kadesh-Barnea (c. 1)
2 Their wanderings (cc. 2, 3)
3 Application of this retrospect (4:1-40)
4 Cities of refuge (4:41-43)

**Second Discourse**
### Review
**(4:44 to 26:19)**
1 The longest of the discourses.
2 Moses reviews the moral, civil, and ceremonial law.
3 Note 5:22, 'and he added no more'; the completeness and finality of Ten Commandments.

**Third Discourse**
### Warning
**(cc. 27, 28)**
1 Instruction as to a solemn ceremony to be performed on entrance into Canaan.
2 Note the altar was built on mount of cursing (27:5). This is gospel.

**Fourth Discourse**
### Covenant
**(cc. 29, 30)**
1 This covenant gives the conditions under which Israel entered the promised land.
2 Observe the emphasis on circumcision of the heart (30:6).

**Fifth Discourse**
### Counsels
**(31:1-23)**
Last counsels of Moses to
1 All Israel (vv.1-6)
2 Joshua (vv.7, 8)
3 Priests (vv.9-15)
4 Jehovah's warning (vv.14-21).
Note the sadness of Jehovah's disclosure in these verses.

**Sixth Discourse**
### Instruction
**(31:24-29)**
1 This is an address to the Levites, concerning the preservation of Deuteronomy.
2 Note RV of v.26 — literally, 'At (or near) the side of the Ark'.

**Seventh Discourse**
### Song
**(31:30 to 32:52)**
A sublime Psalm. Note by v.44 it was sung as a duet by Moses and Joshua, Israel joining in the refrain.

**Eighth Discourse**
### Blessing
**(c. 33)**
A really remarkable prophetic utterance. Note vv.29, 16, 23:
    Saved
    Separated
    Satisfied

**The death of**
### Moses
**(c. 34)**
1 It was a lonely death, as indeed every death is.
2 It was death with a vision.
3 And death in the divine embrace: 'died by the kiss of God' is another rendering.

# 6
# The Book of Joshua

Key word: Possess
Key verses: 11: 23; 21: 44, 45
Theme: The faithfulness of God declared and demonstrated

## Writer
There is no reason to doubt that Joshua wrote this book. The Talmud asserts that Joshua wrote the whole of it except the last five verses, which were probably added by Phinehas (see 24: 33). It certainly was written before the time of David (note 15: 63; David expelled the Jebusites), and while Rahab was still alive (see 6: 25).

## Character
The book is the story of a military campaign led by Joshua, Moses' successor, by which Israel gained possession of Canaan. It is an aggressive book, thus bearing the same relation to the five books of Moses that Acts does to the four Gospels.

## Message
But it is much more than a mere history of a war, interesting though the story is. It has a four-fold message:
1 Its primary message is the faithfulness of God. Study the key verses indicated above. 'He is faithful that promised.' Of course he is: how could he be otherwise? This book declares and demonstrates the faithfulness of our God.
2 It also shows the value of the two foot rule (1: 3), that to enjoy God's good gifts we must definitely appropriate them.
3 Its third message is God's horror and hatred of sin. This war was punitive. The Canaanites were so sunk in sin, so given up to vices of the most awful nature, that God's flaming sword of justice had to be unsheathed.
4 It has a fourth message. This military campaign typifies the warfare of the spirit. The Canaanites represent our lusts, besetting sins and spiritual enemies, and in the record we discover the secret of an all conquering life.

## Notable
One very notable fact concerning this book is its introduction to a new method of teaching. Up to this time God had spoken in dream, vision, or by angelic ministry; now there is the book of the Law written by Moses, and Israel is exhorted to hearken to God's voice in and through that book (see 1:8). This arrangement continues up to date, only the book we have now is much larger than the one Joshua possessed, though just as authoritative. Do we value it enough?

---

## Entrance
### into the promised land (cc. 1 to 5)
1 Lord's summons to Joshua (1: 1-9)
2 Jehovah's appeal to Israel (1: 10-15)
3 People's hearty response (1: 16-18)
4 Rahab and the spies (c. 2)
5 Passage of the Jordan (c. 3)
6 The two memorials (c. 4)
7 Effect of this on enemy (5: 1)
8 Reproach of Egypt rolled away (5: 2-10)
9 New food (5: 11, 12)
10 Their captain (5: 13-15)

Note:
Law, (as represented by Moses) can give sinner no possession (1: 2)
Value of courage (1: 6)
No water was seen by Israel when crossing Jordan. Look at RV of (3: 16)

## Conquest
### of the promised land (cc. 6 to 12)
1 Conquest of Jericho in an unusual way (c. 6) (Note, during the six days, the only sound made was near ark (v. 8), thus drawing attention to the Lord only.)
2 Sin of Achan (c. 7)
3 Conquest of Ai (8: 1-29)
4 The Ceremony on Mount Ebal (8: 30-35) (Note, the altar was built on mount of cursing.)
5 League made with the Gibeonites (c. 9)
6 Victory (a) at Gibeon (10: 1-27)
(b) at Makkedah (10: 28-43)
(c) at Merom (c. 11)
7 List of conquered kings (c. 12)

Note:
Israel's sin of self confidence (7: 3)
In (7: 21), sin is traced in its four stages:
'I saw,' lust of the eyes.
'I coveted,' lust of the mind.
'I took,' act of the will.
'I hid,' act of the hand.

## Division
### of the promised land (cc. 13 to 22)
1 Lord's message to Joshua (c. 13)
2 Division of the land (cc. 14 to 21)
3 The mistake of the two and a half tribes (c. 22)

Note
1 Hebron ('fellowship') became Caleb's because he was out and out for God (14: 14)
2 Caleb's daughter could look well after her own interests (15: 16-19)
3 Joshua's noble and dignified reply (17: 14-18)
4 Joshua was the last to receive his inheritance. Like Caleb he was permitted to choose apart from lot, and he selected a barren place in a barren land no one else would have (19: 50)

## Farewell
### of Joshua, their leader (cc. 23, 24)
1 Joshua's last address (a) to the heads of the people (c. 23)
(b) and to all the people (24: 1-28)
2 Death of Joshua (24: 29-31)
3 Death of Eleazar (24: 33)

Note
1 Genesis begins with God and ends with death; the book of Joshua both begins and ends with death.
2 (24: 33). Priests had no possessions, yet this verse shows Phinehas had — probably a special favour for special service.

# 7
# The Book of Judges

**Key phrase: 'Right in his own eyes'**
**Key verses: 21: 25; 2: 12-16**
**Themes: 1 Our proneness to wander from God**
**2 Results of such spiritual declension**
**3 God's grace in pursuing and restoring backsliders**

## Writer

The writer of this book is unknown. From the phrase found four times in the closing chapters, 'In those days there was no king in Israel' (17: 6; 18: 1; 19: 1; 21: 25), we judge it was written some time after the establishment of the monarchy. Probably it was written by Samuel the prophet, the last judge in Israel, during his partial retirement from the leadership of the people on Saul's becoming king. If so, then with what gusto he would record Gideon's great renunciation (see 8: 22, 23)!

## A sad book

1 The book of Judges — which takes its name from being the history of the 14 Judges who ruled and delivered Israel — covers the period between the conquest of the land (with the death of Joshua) and the judgeship of Samuel and the introduction of the monarchy in Israel.
2 It is the divine record of Israel's repeated departures from God, and of sad national decay, one of the darkest periods of their history.
3 The book of Numbers is a sad book, telling of 40 years wandering through sin; but the book of Judges is far more sad and solemn, for it tells of Israel's failure, not 40 years, but nearly ten times 40. But from the prominence given to Israel's repeated failures one gets the impression that the bulk of the 450 years under the Judges were spent in sin. Such, however, is really not the case, for of the 450 years there were no less than 350 during which the people were loyal to God. This is an astonishing discovery. Of the state of things which existed during this happy period we have a charming picture in the book of Ruth. The erroneous impression is due to the emphasis and detail given of Israel's sin. Even 100 out of 450 years were far too many to spend unfaithful to God. How seriously God viewed these departures!

## Notable

The book is notable for several things. (1) It has two commencements (1: 1; 2: 6). (2) It contains the oldest known parable in the world (9: 8-15). (3) It contains the greatest and grandest battle-song in the world (c. 5). (4) It contains the first record in history of the emergence of a woman into prominence and leadership of a nation (c. 4). Probably she was a widow.

## Message

Being primarily the record of Israel's tragic relapses, this book is (1) a revelation of the perpetual proneness of the human heart to wander away from God. 'Prone to wander, Lord, I feel it; Prone to leave the God I love,' is the bitter confession of many of God's people concerning the waywardness of their hearts. This book shows the awful possibility of spiritual declension after great spiritual blessing. (2) But, thank God, it is not only a book of relapses, it is also a book of deliverance. If there are 7 apostasies and 7 servitudes, there are 7 cries to God and 7 deliverances. God is seen here pursuing and restoring his backslidden people.

## Analysis

At first sight this book seems most disorderly. It certainly is not in chronological order. It ought to begin with 2: 6-9, then c. 1 followed by 2: 10-13, and cc. 17 to 21, and finally by 2: 14 to end of c. 16. But order is heaven's first law, and there is a divine reason for not writing it in chronological sequence. The outline shows this. In the first section we see Israel in dependence upon the Lord; in the second Israel forsaking the Lord, and the bitter results; and in the last we see the abysmal depths to which they sank.

---

**Introductory:**
## Dependence
**upon the Lord**
**(1: 1 to 2: 5; key 1: 1)**
Israel began well but did not continue:
1 Lord consulted and result (1: 1-2)
2 Judah began at home (1: 3, 4)
3 Capture of Adoni-bezek (1: 5-7)
4 Imperfect victories (1: 8-36)
5 The Lord's rebuke (2: 1-5)
(For 'an' RV reads 'the' viz. the Lord himself)

**History of relapses, results, and recovery:**
## Forsaking
**the Lord, and some results**
**(2: 6 to 16: 31; key 2: 12)**
Soon Israel went astray, and 2: 6-23 is a comprehensive summary of their subsequent history:

1st APOSTASY
(3: 1-11)
Conquered by Chushanrishathaim king of Mesopotamia, 8 years.
Delivered and judged by Othniel.

2nd APOSTASY
(3: 12-31)
Conquered by king of Moab and Philistines, 18 years.
Delivered and judged by Ehud and Shamgar.

3rd APOSTASY
(cc. 4, 5)
Conquered by Jabin king of Canaan, 20 years.
Delivered and judged by Deborah and Barak.

4th APOSTASY
(c. 6 to 8: 32)
Conquered by Midian, 7 years.
Delivered and judged by Gideon.

5th APOSTASY
(8: 33 to 10: 5)
Conquered by Civil war, etc.
Delivered and judged by Abimelech, Tola and Jair.

6th APOSTASY
(10: 6 to c. 12)
Conquered by Ammonites, 18 years.
Delivered and judged by Jephthah, Ibzan, Elon, Abdon.

7th APOSTASY
(cc. 13 to 16)
Conquered by Philistines, 40 years.
Delivered and judged by Samson.

**Appendix:**
## Anarchy
**the final result**
**(cc. 17 to 21; key 17: 6)**
Confusion and anarchy
1 In church, or the religious life of the nation (cc. 17, 18).
2 In home life, or the morals of the nation (c. 19).
3 In the State, or the political life of the nation (c. 20, 21).
(Note RV of 18: 30; the first idolatrous priest was Moses' grandson.)

# 8 The Book of Ruth

Key words: Rest, Redeem
Key verses: 1: 9; 3: 1; 4: 4, 6
Theme: Rest through redemption and union

## Literary value

This book, which derives its name from Ruth, the Moabitess, who figures as the chief person in the narrative, is a literary and spiritual gem. The great literary authority of the 18th century, Dr Samuel Johnson, introduced and read it to his friends in a London club as a pastoral which he said he had lately met with, and which they imagined had only just been composed. When they were loud in their praise of its simple and pathetic beauty, he informed them that it was only the story of Ruth, which he had read from a book they all despised — the Bible. There is nothing in human literature more beautiful than Ruth's address to her mother-in-law (1: 16, 17) — it is sublime.

## The book itself

1 Its writer is unknown. It must have been written when the rule of the Judges had ended on the introduction of the monarchy (1: 1), and after the birth of David (4: 22), therefore we conclude that Samuel wrote it. It covers a period of 10 years (1: 4).
2 It is a kind of appendix to the book of Judges. But what a contrast it is to that book! It is like an oasis in a desert.
3 It is notable because it is the only instance in the Bible in which a whole book is devoted to the history of a woman. 'There are two books which bear the name of women: Ruth, a Gentile, who married a Hebrew husband; Esther, a Jewess, who married a Gentile husband.'

## Its purpose

1 One chief purpose of the book is the tracing of the genealogy of David, and of David's Lord. The blood of Ruth ran in the veins of the Lord Jesus.
2 It certainly is a love story, and is designed to set forth the power of a pure love to overcome all difficulties. Strange to say, it is not the story of a romantic love between a young man and a young woman, but the story of a young widow's passionate and devoted love for her mother-in-law.
3 It most assuredly gives a high ideal of wedlock. Married life is treated in 4: 11-17 as a sacred and lofty companionship.

## Its typical value

Typically it is of the utmost value. A greater than Boaz is here. Boaz the kinsman-redeemer is a type of Christ, Ruth being a type of ourselves as Gentiles. This story is a pre-intimation of the calling of the Gentiles. The Moabite, shut out by law (Deut. 23: 3), is admitted by grace. (1) Ruth is a type of Gentile sinners: (a) stranger and afar off (b) poor and needy (c) related to Boaz by marriage, as we are related to Christ by the marriage of our human nature to his divine (d) one nearer kinsman, our fellow-creature, but he cannot help. (2) Boaz a type of Christ: (a) Lord of the harvest (b) 'mighty man of valour' (2: 1, RV marg.). (3) Takes notice of us and treats us kindly (2: 5, etc.). (4) 'And when in penitence we come and lie at his pierced feet, and beseech him to spread over us the crimson mantle of his love, how immediate is his response' (see c. 3). He speaks comforting words and loads us with blessing. (5) Redeeming us, and uniting himself to us, our loneliness ceases, we become fruitful and a blessing to others.

## Message and Analysis

The primary message of the book is that of rest. Though the word is found only twice in it, yet the thought of rest permeates the whole. In the east the position of unmarried women is dangerous and trying — only in the house of a husband can she be sure of respect and protection. Elimelech forsook rest when he left the promised land. To leave Moab for Bethlehem seemed an impossible path to rest, as Naomi gravely and tactfully hinted (1: 11-13), but God's ways are not man's. Ruth found rest through redemption and union with her redeemer. For us there is no rest in the world but in union with our divine redeemer.

---

| Emigration to Moab and result | Return to land of Judah and incidents | Boaz and Ruth | Boaz and Ruth |
|---|---|---|---|
| **Rest Forsaken** | **Rest Desired** | **Rest Sought** | **Rest Secured** |
| (1:1-5) | (1: 6-22) | (cc. 2, 3) | (c. 4) |
| 1 Was this the famine referred to in Judges 6: 3, 4? | 1 After ten (v.4) disastrous years, Naomi decides to return to the land of Israel's rest. | 1 Boaz, a man who had distinguished himself in war, (see RV marg. of 2: 1), was probably absent on military service when Naomi returned, hence his ignorance (2: 5). | 1 Boaz moves in the matter (vv.1-8) |
| 2 Out of will of God there could not be real blessing and prosperity. | 2 Her two daughters-in-law intended to return with her, and actually started (vv.7, 10), but warned, Orpah returned to her people and gods (v.15). | 2 Ruth's act (in c. 3), in creeping softly to his resting place, and nestling under the corner of his long robe, was simply making a legal claim in the approved manner of the time. | 2 Boaz and Ruth married (vv.9-13) |
| 3 Naomi permitted her sons to marry heathen wives. | 3 Reaching Bethlehem, the whole city was moved, yet not one offered hospitality. | | 3 Naomi comforted and happy (vv.14-19) |
| 4 The wives treated their husbands kindly. | 4 Note 'with her' (v.22) — a backslider when restored can be made a blessing to others. | | 4 One of the many fine points of the story is that its concluding sentences are almost wholly devoted, not to the young and happy wife and mother, but to aged Naomi. |

# 9
# The First Book of Samuel

**Key word: Prayed**
**Key verses: 1: 10-27; 7: 5; 8: 6; 12: 19-23**
**Theme: The place for, and the power of prayer in all experiences of life**

### The book
1 Of the six historical books of Israel this is the best known. From infancy the stories of little Samuel (c. 3) and David and Goliath (c. 17) have drawn us, ever with a lasting interest. Though history, it is presented to us in the most attractive garb of biography.
2 It is thus named because Samuel is the prominent figure in it. Undoubtedly he wrote the bulk of it, Nathan and Gad completing it (1 Chron. 29: 29).
3 It gives a history of Israel from the time of Eli to the accession of David to the throne of Israel.

### Notable contents
The contributions of this book to religious vocabulary, theology, and experience, are remarkable.
1 This book has the honour of first giving and using the majestic title 'Lord of hosts' (1: 3). This is the first of the 281 occurrences of that name and title which denotes the God of Israel as the Lord of all the hosts of heaven and earth.
2 The name of Messiah is first found here, a woman having the honour of first using it (2: 10): 'His anointed', literally 'His Messiah' (Septuagint, 'His Christ').
3 This book gives the first of the five precious things in the Old Testament: (1) Word of God (3: 1), (2) Redemption (Psa. 49: 8), (3) The death of his saints (Psa. 72: 14, and 116: 15), (4) Lips of knowledge (Prov. 20: 15), (5) The thoughts of God (Psa. 139: 17).
4 It is here we first find the word 'Ichabod' (4: 21) and 'Ebenezer' (7: 12) also 'God save the King' (10: 24).
5 Here we are told that the original name by which the prophets were known, long before they were called prophets, was 'seers' (9: 9). This is a significant name, indicating their possession of gifts of perception and discernment, as well as a vision of God.
6 It points out that Samuel was the first of the noble line of the writing prophets (3: 20, with Acts 3: 24, and 13: 20); and indicates for the first time the existence of a school of prophets, probably an institution founded by Samuel (10: 5; 19: 20).
7 Its teaching on the Holy Spirit is important. In its pages the Holy Spirit is seen (1) as author and channel of regeneration and a new heart (10: 6, 9), (2) as the author of holy and righteous anger (11: 6), (3) as the inspirer of courage and prudence of speech (16: 13 with 18; 'prudent in matters' is in the RV 'prudent in speech'), (4) and our preservative from evil (16: 14).

### Message
This book bears many messages. (1) It shows the suffering that polygamy brings (1: 6). (2) The disasters that indulgent fatherhood brings (2: 22-25). (3) The peril of mere ritualism and formalism (4: 3, 'it', not the Lord, 'may save us'); (4) of impatience (c. 13) and (5) only partial obedience (c. 15). But the key to THE message of the book is the meaning of Samuel's name, 'asked of God', and the oft occurrence of the words 'prayer' and 'prayed'. It is astonishing how full the book is of prayer. Indeed, it could be viewed as a treatise on prayer vividly illustrated from life. The very name of Samuel is a monument to a prayer presented and granted. Here we see prayer offered at all times. Therefore we take the chief message of the book to be the place for, and the power of prayer in all experiences of life. (1) Samuel given by God in answer to prayer (1: 10-28). (2) Victory was given to Israel through Samuel's prayer (7: 5-10). (3) In sorrow at Israel's rejection of Jehovah as King, evidenced by their request for an earthly king (which rejection began in the days gone by, see Judg. 21: 25), Samuel seeks the Lord in prayer (8: 5, 6). (4) A praying man learns secrets from God (9: 15). (5) Not to pray for Israel Samuel considered to be a sin (12: 19-23). (6) Saul's final rejection seen in the Lord's turning a deaf ear to his prayer (28: 6).

### Analysis
Its contents may be grouped around the names of the three great personages of the book, Samuel, Saul and David.

---

Concerning
## Samuel
**Hannah's request for a son was answered by the gift of Samuel**
**(cc. 1 to 7)**

1 BIRTH:
Given in answer to prayer (c. 1)
Hannah's prophetic prayer (2: 1-11)
2 CALL:
Preserved in a place poisoned by Eli's two wicked sons (2: 12-26)
Grave warning to Eli by unknown prophet (2: 27-36)
Lord revealing himself to Samuel (c. 3)

3 MINISTRY:
Capture of ark and death of Eli (c. 4)
Ark seven months among Philistines (c. 5)
Return of the ark (cc. 5-7)
Victory through prayer (7: 2-17)

Concerning
## Saul
**the people's request for a king answered in the setting apart of Saul**
**(cc. 8 to 15)**

1 CHOSEN:
Samuel takes Israel's request for a king to the Lord in prayer (c. 8)
Saul chosen to be king (c. 9)
Saul anointed king (c. 10)
2 REIGNING:
Saul's first great victory (c. 11)
Samuel's last public address to the nation (c. 12)

3 REJECTED:
Saul's first downward step in the establishment of a standing army (13: 1, 2)
His second downward step (13: 3-14)
A great victory (13: 15; c. 14)
Saul's terrible blunder (c. 15)

Concerning
## David
**anointed king as outcome of Samuel's mourning and prayers**
**(cc. 16 to 31)**

1 ANOINTED:
David selected and anointed (16: 1-13)
2 SERVICE:
Saul's minstrel and armour-bearer (16: 14-23)
Slays Goliath (c. 17)
Love covenant between Jonathan and David (18: 1-7)
Saul's jealousy and attempts to kill David (18: 8-20)

3 EXILE:
David's flight and wanderings (cc. 21 to 30)
Samuel's death (25: 1)
Death of Saul and Jonathan (c. 31)
Note some of David's notable sayings (22: 23; 30: 6, 24)

# 10
# The Second Book of Samuel

Key phrase: 'Before the Lord'
Key verse: 5:12
Theme: Be sure your sin will find you out

## Author
Concerning the authorship of this book, 1 Chronicles 29:29 has something to say, 'The book of Nathan the prophet' and 'the book of Gad the Seer' are supposed to be two of the several books referred to in the Bible that have perished. But the RV is very clear, giving 'history' and 'words' instead of 'book'. Second Samuel was undoubtedly written by Nathan and Gad, two of David's contemporaries.

## Design
This book is almost entirely devoted to a history of David as king. It begins with his accession to the throne, and gives an account of the events during his reign of 40 years. This book is therefore a history of the kingship of David.

## Contents
1 The curious would like this to be noted, that in all the Bible the word 'wench' is found only here (17: 17).
2 The first time a ruler is likened to a shepherd is in 5: 2. 'Feed my people Israel' is literally 'shepherd my people Israel'.
3 It was David who first described a king as 'the Lord's anointed', a phrase which gives a high and exalted conception of kingship (See 1 Sam. 24: 6, with 2 Sam. 1: 14, 16, 21; 2: 4, 7; 3: 39; 5: 3, 17; 19: 10; 22: 51).
4 The incident related in 7: 1-17 teaches that even our good purposes must be brought to God for his approval, a lesson nowhere else in the Bible taught so clearly. How often we err in this respect, making the mistake that Nathan did (7: 3).
5 It contains two notable parables: the parable of the selfish one (c. 12), and the parable of the banished one (14: 1-20).
6 It is in this book (23: 2) that David claimed divine inspiration for his psalms, that even his words came from God.

## Message
1 Its first message is the need of patience and dependence upon God for the fulfilment of his promises (seen in 2: 1; 5: 1-3). Patience is a virtue for which special grace is given.
2 Its second and primary message is that on sin. 'Be sure your sin will find you out' is exemplified in several persons referred to in its narrative (1: 14-16; 2: 8, 9 — Abner acted thus though he knew God's purpose — 3: 9, 13; 3: 27; 4: 11, 12); but more especially in David and his son Absalom. We have horrible details of one awful sin (11: 4; 13: 1-15). How swift was the divine punishment! Yet this book shows how ready God is to forgive (12: 13). But let us not fail to notice that sometimes pardoned sin is punished (12: 14). The whole subsequent history of David is a record of punishment through, and on account of his own sin. This David recognised — see 16: 10; there was little brightness in David's life after his sin.

## Analysis
Though the two books of Samuel were originally one, yet each has characteristics of its own. We have noted that the thought of prayer controls the First book of Samuel. While we have the same prevailing thought here ('Enquired of the Lord' is one of its key-phrases, 2: 1; 5: 19, 23; 21: 1), THE key-phrase is 'Before the Lord'. This means sometimes before the ark of the Lord, but not always (as for instance 5: 3, though the ark was in Gibeah 6: 3. 12; 16 means that he lay before the Lord in his own home). It was David's constant recognition of the presence of God with him always. Note the various attitudes of soul revealed by a study of this phrase, as shown in the following analysis:

---

## DAVID'S TRIUMPHS (cc. 1 to 10)

**1 David, anointed king over Judah, enquired of the Lord**
**(cc. 1 to 4; key 2: 1)**
1 News of Saul's death (1: 1-16)
2 David's elegy he called 'The Song of Bow' (RV of v.18); (1: 17-27)
3 Anointed king of Judah (2: 1-11)
4 Civil war (2: 12 to 4: 12)

**2 David anointed king over all Israel makes league before the Lord**
**(c. 5; key 5: 3)**
1 Crowned king over all Israel (5: 1-5)
2 Jerusalem made the capital (5: 6-16)
3 Victories (5: 17-25)

**3 David consolidating the kingdom —**

**(a) danced before the Lord**
**(c. 6; key 6: 16, 21)**
1 David copied from the Philistines (v.4)
2 God cannot tolerate in his people what he overlooks in the worldling (v.7)

**(b) sat before the Lord**
**(c. 7; key 7: 18)**
1 David's desire to build the Lord's house (vv.1-3)
2 Forbidden (vv.4-13)
3 God covenants to build David a 'house' (v.11)

**(c) preserved by the Lord**
**(cc. 8 to 10; key 8: 6, 14)**
1 Victories (c. 8)
2 Mephibosheth (c. 9)
3 Great victories (c. 10)

---

## DAVID'S TROUBLES (cc. 11 to 24)

**1 David's fall — he lay in penitence before the Lord**
**(cc. 11 to 20; key 12: 16)**
1 Sin (c. 11)
2 Conviction (12: 1-13)
3 Judgment
  (a) Death of babe (12: 14-23)
  (b) Amnon's sin (13: 1-22)
  (c) Absalom's rebellion (13: 23 to 20: 26)

**2 (Appendix) David spake unto the Lord**
**(cc. 21 to 24; key 22: 1; 24: 17)**
1 Enquired of Lord (c. 21)
2 Thanksgiving (c. 22)
3 Last words (c. 23)
4 Sin of numbering Israel (c. 24)

# 11
# The First Book of Kings

Key phrase: 'As David his father'
Key verses: 22: 19; 9: 4-9
Theme: Jehovah the sovereign ruler of Israel: blessing obedient, punishing disobedient, forgiving penitent

## The book

The author of this book is unknown. It certainly was written while the first Temple was still standing (8: 8). Consequently it is probable that Jeremiah, inspired by God, wrote it, incorporating records made by Nathan and Gad (1 Chron. 29: 29), and other writers. It is a history of the kings of Israel and Judah, from David to Ahab and Jehoshaphat, covering a period of from 118 to 125 years.

## Notable contents

1 In 1: 50 and 2: 23 we have the first recorded instances of the use of the horns of the altar as a refuge, the first claims to the right of sanctuary.

2 It gives the first instance of kneeling at devotions (8: 54). Standing was the earliest practice (1 Sam. 1: 26). In fact Solomon stood first before he knelt. (1 Kgs 8: 22). Baal worshippers bent their knees. This explains Judges 7: 5, 7 (why 9,700 of Gideon's troops who bent their knees — proving they had been, or were, worshippers of Baal — were rejected, and only the 300 who lapped were accepted) and 1 Kings 19: 18. However, kneeling at prayer has been sanctified for us by our Lord's use of that posture (Luke 22: 41).

3 It gives the first hint of a new chronology. In 1 Kings 6: 1, the period between the Exodus and the beginning of the Temple building under Solomon, is given as 480 years, whereas it was 573 years. This has proved a stumbling block to many. But devout students of the word have discovered that the difference of 93 years is exactly the length of time covered by the captivities in the book of Judges. This is the solution of the problem. This is God's spiritual chronology. 'During those years Israel was not under Isra-El, not governed by God, but under the heel of the oppressor.' God did not count the years of their captivity. The years lived out of his will are not counted by him. The sin and sins of these years are remembered until confessed, but the years are reckoned by him as wasted and of no account.

4 We have in 5: 5 and 8: 27 the first clear statement in the Old Testament of a wonderfully spiritual conception of God. Observe, the Temple was not built as a house for the Lord, but for the 'name of the Lord'. Pagan temples were intended by their builders for the actual residence of their gods. Solomon knew better. And the expression 'name of the Lord' is a very remarkable one.

5 Notice 5: 3 'his God' and 5: 4 'my God': Solomon gloried in the fact that his father's God had become his God.

6 Observe, (a) that it was the old warrior Joab who first noticed the sound of the trumpet (1: 41). (b) That in 8: 3 we have the only instance of the priests carrying the ark, work the Levites always performed. (c) The description of Jehovah dwelling 'in the thick darkness' (8: 12), which has been a comfort to thousands of tried souls. (Are you in spiritual darkness Christian brother or sister? — Rejoice, for he is with you in that darkness, which only shuts you in with (not from) your Lord.) (d) The unexpected and remarkable conception of Israel's mission in the world (8: 43, 60). Would that Israel had ever remembered this!

## Message

1 This book is written to show the causes of the establishment and decline of the kingdom. It points out that, when loyal to God, Israel flourished, but when Israel departed from God their morals and their kingdom declined. The vision of 22: 19 is very important. God sat as sovereign on his throne, dispensing mercy and grace to the penitent and obedient, but punishment and chastisement to the sinners.

2 Note the new standard, 'as David his father' (3: 3, 14; 9: 4; 11: 4, 33, 38; 14: 8; 15: 3, 11). Man failed to reach even this human standard.

| The Establishment | The Glory | The Disruption | The Decline |
|---|---|---|---|
| **of the kingdom — sad but necessary measures** | **of the kingdom — its unity and splendour** | **of the kingdom — lamentable and fatal schism** | **of the kingdom — its deterioration and decay** |
| **(cc. 1, 2)** | **(cc. 3 to 10)** | **(11: 1 to 12: 24)** | **(12: 25 to 22: 53)** |
| 1 Note 'established' (2: 12, 24, 45, 46) | 1 Note 3: 12, 13; 4: 30; 8: 11 | 1 Note 11: 11; 12: 17 | 1 Note 14: 27, a symbolic act. |
| 2 David prematurely aged (70) (1: 1-4) | 2 Solomon's doubtful alliance (3: 1, 2) | 2 Solomon's apostasy and death (c. 11) | 2 Jeroboam's apostasy and death (12: 25 to 14: 20) |
| 3 David's eldest living son's rebellion (1: 5-9) | 3 First divine appearance to Solomon (3: 5-15) | 3 Accession and folly of Rehoboam (12: 1-15) | 3 Rehoboam and Judah's awful apostasy (14: 21-31) |
| 4 Nathan and Bathsheba's plot (1: 10-31) | 4 The wisdom of Solomon (3: 16-28) | 4 The disruption of the kingdom, Jeroboam becoming king of ten tribes (12: 16-24) | 4 Kings of Judah (15: 1-24) |
| 5 Solomon anointed king (1: 32-52) | 5 The greatness of Solomon (c. 4) | | 5 Kings of Israel (15: 25 to 16: 34) |
| 6 David's last address and death (2: 1-12) | 6 The life's work of Solomon (cc. 5 to 8) | | 6 Ahab and Elijah (cc. 17 to 22) |
| 7 Solomon's execution of various traitors (2: 13-46) | 7 Second divine appearing (9: 1-9) | | |
| | 8 Fame of Solomon (9: 10 to 10: 13) | | |
| | 9 Wealth of Solomon (10: 14-29) | | |

# 12
# The Second Book of Kings

Key phrase: 'According to the word of the Lord'
Key verses: 1: 17; 10: 10; 17: 23; 24: 2
Theme: The fulfilment of the word of the Lord, both sure and certain to saint and sinner

## Originally one book

1 In the original Hebrew, 1 and 2 Kings formed one book, as also did 1 and 2 Samuel, and 1 and 2 Chronicles. They were first divided by the Septuagint translators, when they translated the Old Testament into the Greek language. The explanation given is this: Greek requires at least one third more space than Hebrew, therefore the translators were compelled to divide them, either because the scrolls were of limited length, or to make the scrolls easy to handle.

2 With this in mind, note the perfect order of the two books as one, as pointed out by Dr Bullinger: 'The book begins with King David and ends with the king of Babylon; opens with the Temple built and closes with the Temple burnt; begins with David's first successor on the throne of his kingdom, and ends with David's last successor released from the house of his captivity.'

## Scope of the book

1 This second book of Kings contains the history of Israel and Judah from Ahab to the captivity, a period of about 300 years.

2 The first half of the book is largely taken up with an account of Elisha's ministry of 66 years. This book records 16 miracles by Elisha, whereas Elijah performed only eight. 'The story of Elisha is almost entirely a record of his miracles, and the story of his miracles is almost entirely a record of deeds of beneficence.' (See 2: 14, 21, 24; 3: 20; 4: 1-6, 16, 17, 35, 41, 43; 5: 10, 27; 6: 6, 17, 18, 20; 13: 21.)

3 The second half of the book is taken up with events leading up to the fall of Samaria and captivity of Israel, and the fall of Jerusalem and captivity of Judah.

4 Israel had 19 kings, not one being good, while Judah had 19 kings and one queen, eight of whom were good.

5 Note (a) one of the best of Judah's kings — Hezekiah, was the father of the worst of the kings (c. 21); (b) the remarkable commendation of Josiah (23: 25); (c) how closely the only surviving descendant in the Davidic royal line (11: 1-3), and only existing copy of the Law (22: 8-20), came to perishing.

## Key words

This book abounds with key-words.

1 The phrase 'Man of God' is found in it 36 times, more than any other book in the Bible. God had his brave witnesses in those days.

2 The sad and tragic sentence, 'Did that which was evil in the sight of the Lord' is met with 21 times (3: 2; 8: 18; 12: 2, 11; 14: 24; 15: 9, 18, 24, 28; 16: 2; 17: 2, 17; 21: 2, 6, 15, 16, 20; 23: 32, 37; 24: 9, 19). What they did no doubt was considered right according to earthly standards, but according to the divine rule of faith and practice it was wrong.

3 Thank God, we do meet with the reverse statement, 'right in the sight of the Lord', but only eight times (3: 18; 13: 2; 14: 3; 15: 3, 34; 18: 3; 20: 3; 22: 2).

4 The phrase 'the word of the Lord', and its equivalent, are met with 24 times 1: 17; 4: 44; 7: 1, 16; 8: 19; 9: 26, 36; 10: 10; 25; 15: 12; 19: 21; 20: 4, 16, 19; 22: 13, 16, 18; 23: 2, 3, 16, 24; 24:2

5 Note the prominence given to the Lord's anger (13: 3; 17: 18; 23: 26; 24: 20), and wrath (22: 13, 17; 23: 26).

## Message

These references are listed in full because a study of them gives the message of the book. God's standard of worship and morals had been violated. To meet this Jehovah sent his 'men of God' to warn, and, if possible, lead back to the Lord. They came with a 'Thus saith the Lord'. Failing in this, his anger was roused, and he gave them over to the enemy. In all this he fulfilled his own word.

## Analysis

The book gives graphic descriptions of the Lord's emotions at Israel's base treatment of him — this is shown in the following analysis:

| Closing ministry of ELIJAH | Long ministry of ELISHA | | The passing of ISRAEL | | The passing of JUDAH |
|---|---|---|---|---|---|
| JEHOVAH **Ignored** | JEHOVAH **Derided** | JEHOVAH'S **Anger** | JEHOVAH'S **Compassion** | JEHOVAH'S **Great Anger** | JEHOVAH'S **Fierce Wrath** |
| **(1: 1 to 2: 2)** | **(2: 12-25)** | **(3: 1 to 13: 21)** | **(13: 22 to 16: 20)** | **(c. 17)** | **(18: 1 to 25: 30)** |
| 1 Key 1: 3, 16 | 1 Key 2: 23 | 1 Key 13: 3 | 1 Key 13: 23 | 1 Key 17: 11, 18 | 1 Key 22: 13, 17; 23: 26, with 24: 20. |
| 2 The king's base conduct (1: 1, 2) | 2 Elisha's inducement (2: 12-15) | 2 Elisha's long ministry 66 years. | 2 Kings of Judah: Amaziah (good), Uzziah (good), Jotham (good), Ahaz (bad). | 2 Last king of Israel: Hoshea — bad. | 2 We owe a very great deal to Hezekiah, (see Analysis on Psalms). |
| 3 Elijah's message and deliverance (1: 3, 16) | 3 The 'little children' of v. 23, in RV 'young lads' i.e. young men. | 3 Kings of Judah: Jehoshaphat (good), Jehoram (good), Ahaziah (bad), Joash (good). | 3 Kings of Israel: Jeroboam II, Zechariah, Shallum, Menahem, Pekahiah, Pekah (all bad). | 3 In this chapter we have 'a post mortem enquiry into the diseases that killed a nation'. | 3 Kings of Judah: Hezekiah (good) Manasseh (bad), Amon (bad), Josiah (good), Jehoahaz (bad), Jehoiakim (bad), Jehoiachin (bad), Zedekiah (bad). |
| 4 Elijah's translation (2: 1-11) | 4 'Go up' was a blasphemous reference to Elijah's translation, and, in reality, was deriding the act of Jehovah. | 4 Kings of Israel: Jehoram, Jehu, Jehoahaz, Jehoash (all bad). | | 4 Note the force of v. 23. | |
| 5 King of Israel: Ahaziah, bad. | | | | | |

# 13
# The First Book of Chronicles

**Key phrase: 'Thou reignest over all'**
**Key verses: 5: 20; 12: 18**
**Theme: Jehovah as Sovereign Lord: blessing obedience, punishing disobedience**

## Points to note
(1) Students have noticed a very clear resemblance in style and language between the two books of Chronicles and those of Ezra and Nehemiah. Consequently the authorship of the former is generally ascribed to Ezra; and they must have been written during the Babylonian captivity. (2) While Samuel and Kings concern both kingdoms of Judah and Israel, Chronicles deals only with Judah. (3) The writer has more to say of the Temple and its ritual than of the wars of the kings. It breathes an ecclesiastical atmosphere. (4) Prominence is given to the activities of the Lord on behalf of his people, 4: 9, 10; 5: 20, 22; 11: 14; 12: 18; 14: 2, 11, 15; 18: 13. (5) The justice of the Lord's judgments is declared in 5: 25, 26; 6: 15; 9: 1; 10: 13, 14; 15: 2, 13; 21: 19. (Note — the Lord spoken of as doing this himself.)

## Supplement?
Greek translators gave the books the title — 'Things Omitted' noticing that much information is given not found in the other historical books, and signifying that the books were supplementary to Samuel and Kings. E.g. (1) The genealogy of Judah is enlivened by the episode of Jabez (4: 9, 10) a man of prayer, who because he asked much obtained much. (2) A raid made upon Philistia by part of Ephraim's family, whilst Ephraim (and perhaps Joseph) still lived (see Gen. 50: 23) ended disastrously (7: 21). Perhaps the feud between Israel and Philistines began through this raid made while Israel was yet in Egypt. (3) The erection of a temporary home for the ark by David (15: 1; 16: 1) until the Temple was erected. This will be repeated before the erection of the Temple yet to be built (Acts 15: 16, 17; Ezek. cc. 40 to 46). (4) Age at which the Levites began their ministry, originally 30 (Num. 4: 3), changed to 25 by the Lord (Num. 8: 24), reduced by David to 20 (1 Chron. 23: 27) etc. But these books form much more than mere supplement to other historical books.

## The clue
They form 'an independent work, in which the history of the chosen people is related afresh in a new manner, and from a new standpoint. While the same events are recorded, they are viewed from a different standpoint. In Samuel and Kings we have the facts of history; here we have the divine words and thoughts about these facts. In the former books they are regarded from a man's standpoint; here they are viewed from a divine standpoint' (Dr Bullinger).

## Illustrations
Note in proof, as illustrating this statement: (1) In 1 Samuel c. 31 we are told the Philistines slew Saul; In 1 Chronicles 10: 1-14 that the Lord slew him, and the reason; the Philistines were merely Jehovah's executioners. (2) In Samuel one chapter (2 Sam. 6) is devoted to the removal of the ark to Jerusalem, but in Chronicles three (1 Chron. cc. 13, 15, 16); in Chronicles we are informed why the Lord slew Uzziah, and David's confession (15: 2, 13), not referred to in the other books. (3) Two chapters in Samuel (2 Sam. 11, 12) give particulars concerning David's great sin, but in Chronicles we have no reference to it — in keeping with the character of God, for when he forgives he forgets. (There is reference to David's second great sin (1 Chron. 21: 1), necessary to show what led to the purchase of the Temple site.) (4) In the account of this sin 1 Chronicles 21 reveals the true mover of David, the other books being silent. (5) 2 Samuel 2: 8 gives Ish-bosheth as Saul's son but by 1 Chronicles 8: 33 we learn that he had another name, Esh-baal, *i.e.* 'Man of Baal'. This son probably born after his father's apostasy, his name hints Saul had begun to worship Baal:— the inner and deeper history. (6) In this book Jacob is always called after his spiritual name, Israel (1: 34; 2: 1).

## Message
'The Book of Chronicles is occupied from beginning to end with magnifying God, and giving him his right place in Israel.' Though often ignored and disobeyed, he is still the sovereign Lord: 'Thou reignest over all.' Here we see the Lord active on behalf of those who trusted and served him; here is revealed the true mover to sin; here God's severities are justified, and God glorified in all his ways and works. In spite of the flood of iniquity he is seen sitting as king. By this book Israel's history is seen from the stand-point of heaven. Remembering this, and also that it was written during the Babylonian captivity, students will realise how timely and forceful its message would be.

---

## Genealogies
### (cc. 1 to 9)
The book opens with an outline of primeval history from Adam to David. (Note. Dwelling with the king must come before doing his work [4: 23].)

## Saul
### (c. 10)
Saul's reign is passed over; Saul's overthrow and death are alone recorded.

## David
### (cc. 11 to 20)
1 David and his mighty men (cc. 11, 12)
2 David and the ark (cc. 13, 15, 16)
3 David's prosperity (c. 14)
4 David's desire to build Temple (c. 17)
5 David's victories (cc. 18 to 20)

## Temple
### (cc. 21 to 29)
1 What led to acquisition of Temple site (c. 21)
2 Material prepared for Temple (c. 22)
3 Organization of priests and levites (23: 1 to 26: 23)
4 Organization of officers of state (26: 28 to 27: 34)
5 Closing scenes in David's life (cc. 28, 29)

# 14
# The Second Book of Chronicles

**Key phrase: 'Prepareth his heart to seek God'**
**Key verse: 20: 20**
**Theme: Seeking and serving the Lord: the secret of a vital religion and a life of victory**

## Value of a right standpoint

A party of tourists, after inspecting one of the famous objects of interest in Egypt, were astonished to find that each had a different report to give, until an experienced traveller restored peace by declaring that they were all correct. Conflicting reports were accounted for by different standpoints. In the study of Chronicles everything depends upon securing the right standpoint: in these two books the history of God's people is viewed from the ecclesiastical, and not from the political standpoint; from the divine, and not from the mere human point of view. Let us illustrate this:

## Differences between Kings and Chronicles

1 In Kings 7: 8, we are told Solomon built for Pharaoh's daughter a separate house; Chronicles (2 Chron. 8: 11) informs us it was not in Jerusalem, for Solomon felt an idolatress, though his wife, should not reside in the holy city.
2 Chronicles alone points out that in his apostasy, Jeroboam worshipped not only the golden calves, but also devils (2 Chron. 11: 15).
3 Not one redeeming act in Abijah's reign does Kings record, but in Chronicles (2 Chron. c.13) we have his devout address (vv. 5-12), and cry to God (vv. 14, 18).
4 It is only Chronicles that tells us that good King Asa neglected the Lord in his last illness (2 Chron. 16: 12); that good king Jehoshaphat in spite of 17: 1 entered into a three-fold sinful alliance, (a) Matrimonial (2 Chron. 21: 6) (b) Military (18: 3) (c) Commercial (20: 35); that Athaliah had committed sacrilege (2 Chron. 24: 7); and why the Lord smote Uzziah with leprosy (2 Chron. 26: 16-21).
5 'Hezekiah's reign was divided into two great parts — his military exploits, and the reformation he made in the Temple, and in the worship of God. In 2 Kings (18: 4-6), we have three verses about his reformation, but in 2 Chronicles three chapters (cc. 29 to 31); and with regard to military affairs it is just the reverse — three chapters in Kings are devoted to the secular history, while the religious reformation is dismissed in three verses.'
6 2 Kings c. 21 has much to say concerning Manasseh's wickedness, but it is only in Chronicles (2 Chron. 33: 11-13) we are told of his captivity in Babylon, and his restoration to God and his throne. Because of this, he has been called 'the prodigal of the Old Testament'.
7 Note the remarkable phrase in 2 Chronicles 9: 8: 'The Lord . . . set thee on his throne.' It is on a par with 1 Chronicles 29:23.

## Key phrases and message

1 In reading this book through one phrase is frequently met with, viz. 'Seek the Lord' (7: 14; 11: 16; 14: 4, 7; 15: 2, 4, 12, 13, 15; 17: 4; 19: 3; 20: 3, 4; 22: 9; 26: 5; 30: 19; 31: 21; 34: 3; also see 12: 14; 16: 12). To seek the Lord meant blessing, success, victory.
2 Prayer to, and reliance upon, Jehovah as the secret of success is further brought out in 1: 1; 13: 18; 14: 6, 11; 15: 9; 20: 27; 26: 6, 7; 27: 6; 32: 8, 22. Also see 24: 24; 28: 6, 19; and note 20: 20.
3 A prayerful study of these scriptures leads to the message of the book, viz. that seeking, believing, obeying, serving, and loving the Lord are absolutely requisite to the possession of vital religion and a spiritual and victorious life. Nothing less than this will satisfy the Lord or the deepest cravings of the soul.

## Analysis

1 Though it seems an impossibility to arrange the book in handy divisions, the outline below gives the contents in convenient form, and is in fact a summary of the history of the Lord's people as here narrated.
2 During the reign of Solomon and three years of Solomon's son and successor (cc. 1 to 11), the people were loyal to God, in spite of Solomon's fall, of which Chronicles gives no account. But eventually they 'forsook the Law of the Lord' (12: 1). Swift chastisement followed (vv. 2-4). On Shemaiah the prophet delivering a message, the people humbled themselves (v. 6). Abijah's reign also was not entirely bad (c. 13).
3 The first of the four great religious festivals took place under Asa (c. 15). It was continued by Jehoshaphat (cc. 17 to 20), who sent travelling preachers with the word of God throughout the land (see 17: 7-9, and 19: 4). On the death of Jehoshaphat, under the reign of his son (c. 21), and grandson (c. 22), led by a wicked wife (21: 6), and mother (22: 3), Israel plunged into sin.
4 The second great religious revival took place under Joash, inspired by Jehoiada the priest (23: 1 to 24: 16), but on the death of this good priest, led by the princes of Judah, Joash went astray (vv. 17, 19), even slaying the son of his benefactor who sought to lead him back to the Lord (vv. 20, 22). The dying man's words were twice used by the Lord Jesus (Luke 11: 50, 51, and Matt. 23: 35, 36).
5 The third of these great religious revivals took place under Hezekiah (cc. 29, 30), and the fourth under Josiah (c. 34).
6 Note the strange reward for faithfulness as given in RV of 32:1. Testing often comes after faithfulness.

---

## THE REIGN OF SOLOMON (cc. 1 to 9)

**1 Loyal**
to the Lord.

**2 Forsaking**
the Lord.

## THE KINGS OF JUDAH (cc. 10 to 36)

**1 Seeking**
the Lord.

**2 Serving**
the Lord.

# 15
# The Book of Ezra

**Key phrase: The word of the Lord**
**Key verse: 7: 10**
**Theme: The place and power of the word of God, in the religious, social, and civil life of his people**

## Key

1 The key to the study of this book is the life and master-passion of Ezra, who wrote it about the year 457 B.C.
2 Ezra was a descendant of Hilkiah, High Priest in the reign of Josiah, who found a copy of the Law (read 2 Chron. 34: 14).
3 Though by birth a priest, he was not able to exercise his priestly duties as he was a captive in Babylon. Instead, he gave himself to the study of the word of God (Ezra 7: 10), becoming its great exponent. How little the Law and other divine writings were known to the community at large is seen by a study of 2 Chronicles, Ezra, and Nehemiah. This book records how, mainly through Ezra's ministry, the word of God gained for the first time in the history of Israel and Judah its rightful position.
4 The word of the Lord, as read and expounded by Ezra, came with the force of a new revelation, and wrought wonders in the life of the nation.

## Our debt to Ezra

It has been suggested that the memory of Ezra has scarcely had fair play among Bible lovers. Certainly, we owe a very great deal to him. In addition to his powerful ministry of the word, he wrote 1 and 2 Chronicles, Psalm 119 (which is a striking poem on the word of God), instituted the wonderful system of synagogue worship (the parent of our own), and, assisted by the Great Synagogue, settled the sacred canon of scripture. The revival under Ezra was a revival of Bible study and obedience to the revealed will of God. The fruits of that movement are with us today, though nearly 2,500 year have passed since then.

## Sections

1 Until the third century, Ezra and Nehemiah were treated as a single book, and that may be one explanation of the abrupt close of Ezra.
2 Ezra views the return from exile from the ecclesiastical standpoint, Nehemiah from the civil; Ezra is the book of the Temple building, Nehemiah is the book of the Wall building.
3 It is in two sections, chapters 1 to 6, dealing with the return under Zerubbabel, then, after a break of 57 years, chapters 7 to 10, the return under Ezra.

## Key-phrases

Its key thought is the word of the Lord referred to as 'Word of the Lord' (1: 1), Law (3: 2), Commandments of the God of Israel (6: 14), Book of Moses (6: 18), Law of the Lord (7: 10), Law of Moses (7: 6), Law of thy God (7:14), Words of the God of Israel (9: 4), Commandments of God (10: 3, 5).

## Its message

It gives a clear message on the place and power of the word of God in the religious, social and civil life of his people.

---

## THE RETURN UNDER ZERUBBABEL (about 50,000 people: cc. 1 to 6)

| Return of Israel in fulfilment of the word of the Lord (cc. 1, 2) | Re-erection of altar in obedience to the word of the Lord (3: 1-7) | Rebuilding of Temple in obedience to the word of the Lord (3: 8 to 6: 14) | Restoration of Temple ritual according to the word of the Lord (6: 15-22) |
|---|---|---|---|
| 1 Note 1: 1 | 1 Note 3: 2 | 1 Note 6: 14 | 1 Note 6: 18 |
| 2 As Daniel prophesied in the reign of Darius, probably he had something to do with this proclamation. | 2 Before they thought of homes for themselves, their first thought was the house of God. | 2 Hindrances to all real work for God are to be expected. | 2 About 23 years passed between the return of the exiles and the completion of the Temple. |
| 3 The very heathen assisted by their gifts (1: 6). | 3 And they did not begin with the walls or Temple, but the altar. | 3 The church must not have the help of the world (4: 1-3). | 3 V. 17 is a proof that representatives of *All* the tribes returned (see 8: 35). |
| 4 While only 74 Levites returned, 4,000 priests did so. | 4 The atoning work must come first, and be at the heart of every real live movement. | 4 This opposition disheartened them, hence the need of Haggai's message (6: 14). (Read Haggai here) | |

## THE RETURN UNDER EZRA (about 2,000 people: cc. 7 to 10)

| The student of the word of God commissioned (cc. 7, 8) | Repentance and reform through the word of the Lord (c. 10) |
|---|---|
| 1 Note 7: 10 | |
| 2 How Ezra loved the word! | 3 Have *I* learned yet to tremble at the word of God ? (v. 4) |
| 3 By 7: 12 we note how impressed the king was with Ezra's love and estimate of God's word. May we, too, so live that others might learn to respect God's Book! | 4 Let us study on our knees, Ezra's touching prayer and confession (vv. 5-15). |
| 4 Note Ezra's loyalty to God and jealousy for God's glory (8: 21, 22). | **Repentance and reform through the word of the Lord (c. 10)** |
| **A great trembling at the word of the Lord (c. 9)** | 1 Note 10: 5 |
| 1 Note 9: 4 | 2 Here we see the word of God at work, producing genuine repentance, and leading to separation. |
| 2 On his arrival he found things even worse than he expected. | 3 In this book we have separation — from Babylon (c. 1), from worldly help (c. 4), from leaning on the arm of flesh (8: 21-23), from sinful alliance (10: 10, 11). |

# 16 The Book of Nehemiah

**Key words: Prayer, Work**
**Key verses: 1: 4; 6: 3**
**Theme: Prayer, pains, and perseverance, the conditions of successful work for God**

## Introduction

1 The Book of Nehemiah is largely autobiographical, and the last historical book of the Old Testament.

2 The book is a striking revelation of the character of Nehemiah. He was born (probably of the royal house of Judah) in exile, and became cup-bearer to the mighty king, Artaxerxes. Though comfortably situated in Shushan, his circumstances all that could be desired, his heart was in the ruined city of his fathers.

3 This life, of ease, luxury and certain substantial advancement, he renounced at the call of God for a life of toil, danger, and the heart-breaking work of a reformer. Have we given him the honour he deserves for his 'great acceptance'?

4 This book reveals him as 'a man of patriotism and courage — fearless, enthusiastic, and enterprising, a man of prayer and hard work, one who feared God, and sought his blessing'. 'His character is without blot.'

5 Between Ezra and Nehemiah there is an interval of about twelve years. Nehemiah's administration covered a period of 36 years, and was marvellously successful, in spite of incessant and bitter opposition. The book begins and ends with prayer.

## Message

1 As key words and key verses suggest, it has a peculiar and opportune message for Christian workers. It points out that the conditions of success in work for God are prayer, pains, and perseverance.

2 Nehemiah is revealed as a model worker for God:

(a) A man with a heart at leisure from himself to sorrow over the sad state of Zion (1: 4).

(b) A man of prayer at all times, and under all circumstances, thus living in fellowship with God (1: 5-11; 2: 4; 4: 4, 9; 5: 19; 6: 9, 14; 13: 14, 22, 29, 31).

(c) A man determined to become personally acquainted with the true state of affairs (2: 12).

(d) A man full of self-denying labours for the cause of God (2: 5).

(e) A man able to inspire others to work (2: 17, 18) as well as to work himself (4: 23).

(f) A man with a glorious conception of the sacredness and nobility of work for God. (Note 6: 3; to leave the work he was engaged in, even to meet the great ones of the district, he considered to be a 'coming down').

(g) A man undismayed and undisturbed by opposition from without and within.

(h) A man ever ready to give God all the praise for any wisdom he displayed (7: 5, with 2: 12).

---

## The events which led to Nehemiah's appointment as governor of Judah

**(1: 1 to 2: 11)**

1 Scene laid in the royal palace.

2 In December, from his brother, he learns of the sad state of Jerusalem (1: 1-3).

3 This news led him to prayer (vv.4-11). Note 'God of Heaven'.

4 'And to the prayer of thy servants' (v.11) proves he was the moving spirit in a little circle of praying friends.

5 After four months prayer, comes enquiry and commission of the king (2: 1-10).

---

## The building of the wall in spite of many difficulties

**(2: 12 to 6: 19)**

1 After resting three days he privately inspected the ruins at night (2: 12-16).

2 Then inspires the people to work (2: 17-20).

3 Names, and account of work done (c. 3).

4 Nehemiah had six forms of opposition from the enemy: grief (2: 10), laughter (2: 19), wrath (4: 1), mocking (4: 1), conflict (4: 8), subtlety (6: 2, 3).

5 More dangerous still, opposition from friends within: discouragement (4: 10-23), selfishness (c. 5).

6 Wall finished in 52 days.

7 No account of what he himself did.

---

## Nehemiah's wise organization and preparation, in view of his return to Babylon

**(cc. 7 to 12)**

1 Before the stirring dedication of the finished wall (12: 27-43),

2 Came arrangements for guarding wall and city (7: 1-4);

3 Census (7: 5-73; cc. 11, 12);

4 And calling of a great and remarkable convention for reading and exposition of the Word (cc. 8 to 10). (Only reference to 'pulpit' in the Bible 8: 4.)

---

## Certain reforms accomplished after his return from Babylon

**(c. 13)**

1 After twelve years' absence at the court of Persia, Nehemiah returns to find need of another reformation.

2 Note the High Priest's sad fall, through worldly alliance (13: 4).

3 Nehemiah deals drastically with the offenders (vv.8, 28).

4 Sabbath rest established; wrong marriage ties dissolved.

# 17
# The Book of Esther

**Key phrase: 'For such a time as this'**
**Key verse: 4: 14**
**Theme: The reality of the divine providence**

## Problem

1 It is said that Luther declared himself so hostile to the book of Esther that he wished it did not exist. Many today have the same view. Certainly the book is a problem, and bristles with difficulties. At first sight the tone of the book does seem to be 'of a wholly secular character, and to deprive it of any claim to be regarded as a book of spiritual teaching, and still less to be entitled to a place in the volume of holy scripture'.
2 Note (a) God's name is never mentioned, though the heathen king's name occurs 187 times. (b) It is never quoted in the New Testament. (c) It makes no reference to prayer, or any of the sacred observances of the Jewish Law. (d) The superstitious habit of observing lucky days, and that by a heathen, is its only approach to the supernatural.

## Fact

1 Before hastily condemning it we should enquire the view of the Jewish people concerning it, and whether we really understand it or not.
2 It is a fact that not only was this book accepted as part of the canon, but it was regarded by many of the Jews as peculiarly sacred. It held a place in their view second to the five books of Moses.

## Solution

1 The very absence of the name of God is its chief beauty, and should by no means be considered a blemish.
2 Matthew Henry says: 'If the name of God is not here his finger is.' This book is, as Dr Pierson called it, '*The Romance of Providence.*' By providence we mean that in all the affairs and events of human life, individual and national, God has a part and a share. But that control is a secret and hidden one. Hence in this wonderful story, which teaches the reality of the divine providence, the name of God does not appear, 'only the eye of faith sees the divine factor in human history; but to the attentive observer all history is a burning bush aflame with the mysterious presence'.
3 The Talmud gives Deuteronomy 31: 18 as another reason why God's name is not mentioned. Because of their sin, God had hidden his face from Israel. Yet, though hiding his face, he was not forgetful or unconcerned about his people, though he did all under a veil.
4 It has also been suggested that this book is an extract from the official documents of the Persian court (2: 23). This would account for its omission of the name of God, and for its minute details.

## Author

1 Nothing can be said dogmatically concerning its authorship. Augustine ascribed the book to Ezra; the Talmud, to the Great Synagogue.
2 One possibility is that Mordecai himself wrote the book — see 9: 20.

## Analysis

Curiously, all the events of the book circle around three Feasts; therefore it falls naturally into three divisions:

## The Feast of Ahasuerus
### and its sequel

(cc. 1, 2)
1 A feast which lasted six months (1: 1-4)
2 Followed by a seven days' feast (1: 5-8)
3 The Queen's noble refusal and deposition (1: 9-22)
4 Between cc. 1, 2, the king made his historic attack on Greece with an army of five millions, suffering a terrible defeat.
5 Selection and enthronement of Esther (2: 1-20)
6 Mordecai saves the life of the king (2: 21-23)
(Note. 'Esther' is Persian, meaning 'The Star of the East'. Her Hebrew name was Hadassah, meaning 'Myrtle'.)

## Events leading up to
## The Feast of Esther
### and its sequel

(cc. 3 to 7)
1 Mordecai's refusal to worship a descendant of the Agag whom Samuel slew (3: 1, 2)
2 The court busy-bodies tell Haman (3: 3, 4)
3 Haman's conspiracy (3: 5-15)
4 The fasting of the Jews (4: 1-4)
5 Mordecai's message to Esther (4: 5-14)
6 Esther's fast (4: 15-17)
7 Esther interviews the king (5: 1-8)
8 Haman plots to slay Mordecai (5: 9-14)
9 King's sleepless night and result (c. 6)
10 Esther's feast and result (c. 7)

## Institution of
## The Feast of Purim
### and its sequel

(cc. 8 to 10)
1 Esther's intercession and stratagem to save life of Israel (c. 8)
2 Day of self defence (9: 1-19)
3 The Feast of Purim instituted, which has been observed ever since by the Jews (9: 20-32)
4 The greatness of Mordecai (c. 10)
(Note: 'Sending portions' (9: 19). It is believed our observance of Christmas has been largely moulded on the custom at Purim of sending portions.)

# 18
# The Book of Job

**Key word:** Trial
**Key verses:** 1: 9 with James 5: 11
**Theme:** Trials and suffering sometimes come for our education, not always as chastisement

**Opinions**
In the opinion of many, the book of Job is the most remarkable book in Holy Writ. Tennyson called it 'the greatest poem, whether of ancient or modern literature'. Luther regarded it as 'more magnificent and sublime than any other book of scripture'. Carlyle wrote: 'I call that (Job) one of the grandest things ever written with pen.'

**Date**
It is the most ancient book known. It must have been written about the time of Jacob. Note (1) total silence of the disputants on the miracles attending the Exodus. (2) Length of Job's life places him in the patriarchal times. (3) Job acted as high priest in his family, which was not allowed after the Exodus. (4) Eliphaz was descendant of Esau's eldest son called Eliphaz, who had a son called Teman (Gen. 36: 10, 11).

**Author**
Unknown. Job 32: 16 (note the 'I') seems to show that Elihu wrote it. Though the book is written in poetical form (with the exception of the first two chapters, and part of the last)

Job and the others were actual beings, so it is fact not fiction.

**Message**
Incidentally it shows how remarkably full were the theological knowledge and intellectual culture of the patriarchal age. Almost every important doctrine is found therein, in addition to scientific truths only fully discovered in our own time. But the message of the book is on the mystery of suffering. All suffering was thought to be on account of personal sin. Yet the apparent failure of God to reward his servants and punish his enemies as they deserved was a problem which always tried the faith of Old Testament saints. Because Job suffered so heavily his friends were sure he must have sinned dreadfully. But while this book does not solve, it gives additional and welcome light upon, the mystery of suffering and pain. It proves that, as in Job's case, suffering is sent, not as chastisement, but as a test, a revealer of character, and to educate and instruct. The ancients asked: 'How can a man be godly if he suffers?' We Christians say: 'How can a man be God-like if he knows nothing of suffering?'

## Job before the trial
(1:1-5)

JOB'S —
1 Place: Uz, in Lamentations 4:21, identical with Edom.
2 Purity (v.1)
3 Prosperity (vv.2-4)
4 Popularity (see c. 29)
5 Piety (v.5)
(Note. v.4 — sons had homes of their own. v.5 — Job sought access to God through sacrifice.)

## Satan and the mystery of pain
(1:6 to 2:10)

SATAN'S —
1 Admission into the court of heaven (v.6)
2 Restlessness (v.7)
3 Power: its extent and limit.
4 Theory: Job good only for what he could get.
5 Declaration: suffering would annihilate Job's piety.
6 Theory proved wrong.
(Note. 'The Sons of God' (v.6) were angels (38: 7).)

## The end of Job's patience
(2:11 to 3:26)

Here ends Job's patience; here begins Job's complaining. Though he cursed not God, he cursed the day of his birth, placing among his curses what Satan placed among his blessings: (1: 10 with 3: 23).
(Note. In 2: 13 the period of very great mourning.)

## Fruitless philosophical discussion
(cc. 4 to 37)

1 A sameness in the arguments: all suffering is a result of personal sin. Job therefore a great sinner.
2 In first discourses this is elaborated; each ends with an appeal to Job to repent.
3 In the second series each deals with sufferings and end of the wicked. The third resembles the first.
4 Eliphaz backs arguments by lessons from a dream or vision, Bildad from proverbs (8: 2-13), Zophar from experience and reason.
5 Job holds same views, yet protests innocence, and in c. 21 argues the wicked often prosper.
6 Elihu shows (c. 33) that suffering may be God's discipline — nearest the truth.

## Jehovah and the mystery of suffering
(cc. 38 to 41)

1 'We are struck by what God does not say. Hitherto the book has been one long argument, but there is no argument here . . .
The mysteries of divine providence are not to be settled by logic. Rest does not enter the heart by way of intellectual powers.'
2 'Job's thoughts were turned from himself to God. If he were unable to explain ordinary and well known facts (of natural history and science) how could he explain the mystery of God's ways.'
3 'The fact that God did not explain the mystery of suffering teaches us that he wants our confidence.'

## Job and 'the end of the Lord'
(c. 42)

What was the Lord's purpose in permitting suffering to Job?
1 To reveal Job's character.
2 As an object lesson to others — 'God's Blackboard'.
3 To bring out hidden sin, of which Job was unconscious, namely — self-righteousness.
(Note. V.6 is always the language of the true penitent. Note, too, the force of v.10.)

# 19
# The Book of Psalms

Key word: Worship
Key verse: 29: 2
Theme: 'Worship the Lord in the beauty of holiness'

## A testimony

All devout readers of the Psalms can appreciate the glowing testimony of C. H. Spurgeon, written upon completion of his great commentary on the Psalms, which took twenty years: 'A tinge of sadness is on my spirit as I quit *The Treasury of David*, never to find on this earth a richer storehouse, though the whole palace of Revelation is open to me. Blessed have been the days spent in meditating, mourning, hoping, believing, and exulting with David. Can I hope to spend hours more joyous on this side of the golden gate? The book of Psalms instructs us in the use of wings as well as words: it sets us both mounting and singing.'

## What it is

The book of Psalms is a collection of 150 spiritual songs or poems, many of which were set to music for the Tabernacle and Temple worship. 'They set forth the attitude of the soul in the presence of God when contemplating past history, present experience, and prophetic hope.' 'Every Psalm is a direct expression of the soul's consciousness of God.'

## Authors

These sacred and inspired poems were written by various persons: Moses wrote one (90); David composed seventy-three Psalms; Sons of Korah eleven; Asaph twelve; Heman one (88); Ethan one (89); Hezekiah ten; the remainder being anonymous.

## Analysis

1 From ancient times the book was always understood to be in five sections, each ending with a doxology (see RV).
2 But why the book should be thus divided has been for ages a puzzling problem.
3 It has been thought that in book 1 we have a collection by David of the Psalms he composed; in book 2 additional Psalms for use in the Temple, compiled by Hezekiah; in book 3 a compilation by Josiah; and in books 4 and 5 a collection by Ezra and Nehemiah. But this explanation is not wholly satisfactory.
4 It is quite certain that the Psalms are not arranged in chronological order, else the oldest (90) would be the first.
5 The proper solution is found in a right understanding of a very ancient Jewish statement: 'Moses gave to the Israelites the five books of the Law; and corresponding with these David gave them the five books of the Psalms.'
6 The whole book thus forms a poetical pentateuch. This is splendidly brought out in 'The Companion Bible' as follows:

## BOOK 1:
### Psalms 1 to 41

**Corresponding with Genesis**

### Man: his state of blessedness, fall and recovery

1 Man in a state of blessedness (1)
2 'He is seen (2 to 8) fallen from his high position of blessing, at enmity with God,
3 That enmity culminating in anti-christ (9 to 15);
4 But finally blessed by the gracious work of the man Christ Jesus' (16 to 41).
(Key words: 8: 4; 10: 18)

## BOOK 2:
### Psalms 42 to 72

**Corresponding with Exodus**

### Israel's Ruin, Redeemer, Redemption

**(42-49; 50-60; 61-72 respectively)**
'In the Genesis book man is the central thought; in this Exodus book, it is the nation of Israel. It opens with the "cry" from the depth of ruin and oppression, as Exodus does; and it ends with the king reigning over the redeemed nation (Psalm 72), brought "again the second time" from the four corners of the earth, as it was brought the first time out of Egypt.'

## BOOK 3:
### Psalms 73 to 89

**Corresponding with Leviticus**

### The Sanctuary

'In this the counsels of God are seen in relation to the sanctuary, which is mentioned or referred to in nearly every Psalm of this third book. The sanctuary is seen from its ruin to its establishment in the fulness of blessing.'

## BOOK 4:
### Psalms 90 to 106

**Corresponding with Numbers**

### The Earth

As Numbers is the 'Book of the Wilderness', or earth, so in this fourth section the earth is the central thought. 'Blessing for the earth is needed (Psalms 90 to 94), anticipated (95 to 100), and enjoyed (101 to 106).'
(Its first Psalm (90) was written during the wanderings in the wilderness.)

## BOOK 5:
### Psalms 107 to 150

**Corresponding with Deuteronomy**

### The Word of God

All the teaching of this fifth section is grouped around the word of God. 'The book opens with Psalm 107 which gives the key. "He sent his word and healed them," while Psalm 119 is the great Psalm of the whole book.'

# 20
# The Book of Proverbs

Key phrase: Words to rule life
Key verse: 9: 10
Theme: Godliness is intensely practical

## Antique method of teaching

Proverbial teaching is one of the most ancient forms of instruction. From earliest historical times every nation has had its proverbs. This method was well adapted to times when books were few and costly, as the clear crisp sentences were so easily memorised. But even today, in this age of learning, proverbs are household words, and exert a mighty influence.

## The home of proverbs

Without doubt, the East is the original home of proverbs. Nearly all the proverbs of Europe can be traced to the East, so our wise men declare. The finest collection of proverbs in the world is the book bearing that name in the Bible — an Eastern book. But this book is more than a collection of human wisdom: it is divine wisdom, intended to rule our daily life. And we neglect it at our peril. It is designed to teach us how intensely practical godliness is.

## Authors

This book, written by inspiration of God, had a variety of human authors. Only in cc. 10 to 19, and 25, 26 have we proverbs conceived and written by Solomon. In 1: 6 to 9: 18; 19: 20 to 24: 34 we have 'The words of the wise' (see 1:6; 22: 17; c. 24 RV), i.e. words taught Solomon by his teachers. And in cc. 30, 31, we have the words of Agur and Lemuel. Out of the 3,000 proverbs Solomon 'spake' (1 Kgs 4: 32), he was led to select and 'set in order many' (Eccles. 12: 9). Years afterward 'the men of Hezekiah, king of Judah,' (Prov. 25: 1) made a further selection from that vast store, preserved no doubt in the royal library. The book of proverbs was then complete as we have it today.

## Topical system of study

The best method of studying this book is the topical method. Trace all this book has to say on Fools, Wise Man, Heart, Sluggard, Righteous, etc., and discover a mass of teaching. Here is a pattern-study on the Fool:
(a) A Fool Defined: One who trusts in his own heart (28: 26).
(b) A Fool's Belief: His way is right (12: 15); he detests the thought of departing from evil (13: 19). (c) A Fool's Acts: 1. Hates anything that makes him feel small (1: 7); 2. No self-control (12: 16); 3. His words are very foolish (12: 23); 4. Makes a mock at sin (14: 9); 5. Thinks little of his mother (15: 20); 6. No concentration of thought or purpose (17: 24); 7. Food (15: 14); 8. No delight (18: 2); 9. Mouth gets him into trouble (18: 6-7). (d) How to Treat a Fool: (13: 20; 23: 9; 26: 4 and 5). (e) A Fool's End: (3: 35; 11: 29 with Luke 12: 20). (f) A Fool's Saviour: Learn the A.B.C. of Wisdom, i.e. 'the fear of the Lord'. And let the Lord be 'made unto your Wisdom'.

## Analysis

Solomon 'set in order' his collection of Proverbs; but is any 'order' to be discerned in it? At the first glance it appears to be a jumble. But there is no disorder in any divine book. A second glance reveals three divisions, marked by the phrase 'The Proverbs of Solomon' (1: 1; 10: 1; 25: 1). But on a more careful inspection of these three divisions, striking differences are observed, especially in the pronouns — in some portions the pronouns are in the second person, in others the third person. This and other facts have led Dr Thirtle and others to decisive conclusions, viz. that when you have the pronouns in the second person, you have proverbs FOR Solomon, taught him by his teachers, but when you have pronouns in the third person, you have proverbs taught BY Solomon.

## Introduction
(1: 1-5)
1 Object and result of a study of this book.
2 Who will take heed?

## PART 1: Proverbs for Solomon
(1: 6 to 9: 18)
Fourteen addresses, all introduced by the phrase 'My son' (1: 8, 10, 15; 2: 1; 3: 1, 11, 21; 4: 1, 10, 20; 5: 1; 6: 1, 20; 7: 1).

## PART 2: Proverbs by Solomon
(10:1 to 19:19)
Not the second person (thy, thee) but the third person (he, him, his, they, them).

## PART 3: Proverbs for Solomon
(19: 20 to 24: 34)
Six addresses beginning with the formula 'My son' (19: 27; 23: 15, 19, 26; 24: 13, 21).

## PART 4: Proverbs by Solomon
(cc. 25, 26)
Copied by men of Hezekiah from the royal library.

## PART 5: Proverbs for Solomon
(cc. 27 to 29)
Begins without any formal introduction.
Note again 'My son' (27: 11).

## PART 6: Proverbs by Agur
(c. 30)
V.4 is 'God Almighty's great conundrum spoken out of eternity into time.'

## PART 7: Proverbs by a Mother
(c. 31)
Sundry wise advice, and also praise of a virtuous wife.

# 21
# The Book of Ecclesiastes

Key phrase: 'Under the sun'
Key verse: 12: 13
Theme: Apart from God life is full of weariness and disappointment

## Indispensable
1 That this book has always been a favourite book with atheists startles us. It is said that Voltaire appealed to it in support of sceptical philosophy. No one can deny that it contains statements at variance with the remainder of Bible teaching, and gives approval to things Christians denounce. Read 1: 15; 2: 24; 3: 3, 4, 8, 11, 19, 20; 7: 16 and 17; 8: 15.
2 Even if we decide that the Book is contradictory and impossible to understand we cannot dispense with it, for it is quoted largely in the New Testament; 7: 2 in Matthew 5: 3, 4; 5: 2 in Matthew 6: 7; 6: 2 in Luke 12: 20; 11: 5 in John 3: 8; 12: 14 in 2 Corinthians 5: 10; 5: 1 in 1 Timothy 3: 15; 5: 6 in 1 Corinthians 11: 10.

## Scientific facts
Then it contains scientific statements astoundingly accurate. 'There is a danger in pressing the words in the Bible into a positive announcement of scientific fact, so marvellous are some of these correspondences. But it is certainly a curious fact that Solomon should use language entirely consistent with discoveries such as evaporation and storm currents (1: 6, 7).' Who taught Solomon to use terms that readily accommodate such facts as: the movement of the winds, which seem to be so lawless yet are ruled by laws as positive as those which rule the growth of the plant; and evaporation, by which the waters that fall on the earth are continually raised again, so that the sea never overflows? 12: 6 is a poetic description of death. How aptly the 'silver cord' describes the spinal marrow, the 'golden bowl' the basin which holds the brain, the 'pitcher' the lungs, and the 'wheel' the heart. 'Without claiming that Solomon was inspired to foretell the circulation of the blood, twenty-six centuries before Harvey announced it, is it not remarkable that the language he uses exactly suits the facts — a wheel pumping up through one pipe to discharge through another?' (following Dr Pierson)

## Character
1 There is no doubt that Solomon was its author (1: 1), or that it is the dramatic autobiography of his life and experience when he got away from God, and tried various methods of securing happiness. This book had its origin in the sad backsliding of Solomon.
2 Did Solomon get right again? Was he ever restored? The concluding verses of this book seem to declare decisively in the affirmative.

## Key word
1 It abounds with key-words. 'Under the sun' occurs twenty-nine times; 'Vanity' thirty-seven; 'Under the heaven' three; 'Upon the earth' seven.
2 Its true key-phrase is 'Under the sun'. It has been well called 'the book of the natural man'. It is significant that the covenant title 'Jehovah' is not used in the book, which refers only to man in relation to his Creator. There is no 'Thus saith the Lord' in the book. It is simply a work of argument and an appeal to reason, giving particulars of a long experiment in search of satisfaction and happiness without God.
3 But the Christian man is not merely 'under the sun', but is above the sun, 'seated' with Christ in the heavenly places. And what the man 'under the sun' states to be impossible, the man of God above the sun knows and expresses to be gloriously possible (1: 15 being answered by God in Isaiah 40: 4 and 42: 16, with Luke 3: 5, and 13: 13 — note printed heading to this page in AV/KJV — also Phil. 2: 15; and 1: 9 being answered in 2 Cor. 5: 17, Rev. 21: 5).

## Message
The message of the book is that, apart from God, life is full of weariness and disappointment. It is well that Ecclesiastes is followed by the Song of Solomon, for the one is the complement of the other. 'In Ecclesiastes we learn that without Christ we cannot be satisfied, even if we possess the whole world — the heart is too large for the object. In the Song of Solomon we learn that if we turn from the world and set our affections on Christ, we cannot fathom the infinite preciousness of his love — the Object is too large for the heart.' The Analysis is as follows:

## The Problem
(1:1-3)
How be satisfied and happy without God?

## The Experiment
(1: 4 to 12: 12)
He sought satisfaction in Science (1: 4-11), but he noted a horrid sameness in nature; in
Mere wisdom and philosophy (1: 12-18), but all to no purpose; in
Pleasure (2: 1-11), in mirth, drinking, building, great possessions, wealth and music, but found all empty; he tried
Materialism (2: 12-26), by living merely for the present, even trying
Fatalism (3: 1-15), and
Deism (3: 16 to 4: 16), but found all wanting. He tried

Religion (without God) (5: 1-8), and
Wealth (5: 9 to 6: 12), but without satisfaction. Finally he tried
Morality (7: 1 to 12: 12). Here, in a purer atmosphere, he gets on to a higher platform: but even morality did not satisfy.

## The Conclusion
(12: 13 to 14: 14)
1 'Solomon stands before us, by turns, as the man of science, and the man of pleasure, the fatalist and materialist, the sceptic, epicurean and stoic, with a few earnest and enlightened interludes, till in the conclusion of the whole matter, he sloughs the last of these lying vanities, and emerges to our view the noblest style of man, the penitent and the believer.'

2 Note. 12: 13 — literally, 'This is the whole of man,' i.e. to do this means that you are a whole, not a half man, therefore holy.
3 God alone can satisfy.

# 22
# The Song of Solomon

**Key word: Love**
**Key verse: 8: 6**
**Theme: The Communion of Christ with his people; its necessity, condition and result**

## Misunderstood
This is one of the most misunderstood books of the Bible. Many Christians even question its right to be in the sacred library.

## Opinions
Before condemning it, note; The Jews have ever held this song in the greatest esteem, reckoning it amongst the holiest of books. They compared Proverbs to the outer court of the Temple, Ecclesiastes to the Holy Place, and the Song of Solomon to the Holiest of all. Jonathan Edwards, of revered fame, writes: 'The whole book of Canticles used to be pleasant to me, and I used to be much in reading it . . . and found, from time to time, an increased sweetness that would carry me away in my contemplation.' The fact is, the most spiritually minded men the world has ever known have revelled in its pages.

## Why misunderstood?
Unkind critics do not remember that it is (1) Poetry, not prose; we give poets a wide license. (2) An *oriental* poem. Orientals revel in figures of speech we abhor: nothing here would offend the most modest oriental. (3) It is a *parable*, therefore the question is not one of inspiration, but of interpretation. (4) It was sung annually on the eighth day of the Passover feast: therefore only those who know the Lord Jesus as their Passover Lamb can possibly understand it.

## What is it?
1 Probably the book had basis in an actual story of earthly love, the story of Solomon and a maid of Shulam. One writes: 'It is a record of the real history of a humble and virtuous woman engaged to be married to a young man of like humble circumstances, who was tempted to transfer her affections to one of the richest and most famous men that ever lived. It celebrates the victory of chaste love in humble life over all the attractions of worldly advantage, and all the allurements of courtly grandeur. It is a revelation of the chaste and virtuous love which no splendour can dazzle, and no flattery seduce.'
2 That is only background and framework. Dr Duff says: 'We find here startlingly shadowed forth, in the impassioned strains of loftiest oriental metaphorical imagery, often far too glaring for colder occidental habitudes of thought and feeling, the loving relationship, transporting fellowship, and warmly affectioned intercourse between Emmanuel — the God-man — and individual human souls.' Mrs Penn Lewis wrote: 'In *The Song of Songs* we have unveiled to us the heart-history of the redeemed who is led on to know the Lord, veiled in language to be understood only by the teaching of the eternal Spirit; we see how the heavenly Bridegroom woos the soul for whom he died, leads it on from one degree of union to another, draws it with the cords of love to forsake itself and its own life, and then causes it to know, in real experience, one life with him.'

## Three stages of love
(1) At first the ruling thought of the soul is 'My beloved is mine and I am his' (2: 16). At this stage we think chiefly of Christ as ours, and in some way for our pleasure. (2) Then we come to 'I am my beloved's, and my beloved is mine' (6: 3). His ownership takes first place in our thoughts. (3) At last we come to 'I am my beloved's and his desire is toward me' (7: 10), where the word 'mine' is altogether dropped in the perfect assurance that to be his includes all.

## Analysis
It can be divided into five sections, and in every section but two, (3rd and 5th), we have recorded absences between bride and bridegroom, and the result of such absences, terminating in the union and delight of the severed ones.

## (1) 1:1 to 2:7

(1: 1) Introduction — best of all the songs of Solomon.
(1: 2) Desire for kiss of communion.
(1: 3) Bridegroom absent, yet name fragrant; his love valued above all earthly joys.
(1: 4-6) Confession of weakness, unworthiness; remembers past mercies.
(1: 7) Longs to find beloved, though he hides himself.
(1: 8) He directs her how to find him.
(1: 9 to 2: 2) At last the king reveals himself; his glowing description of bride, her description of him,

(2: 3-7) Testimony of bride showing she is now satisfied.

## (2) 2:8 to 3:5

We again have absence between bride and bridegroom (vv.8, 9); bride asleep (v.10); cry of bridegroom for his beloved (vv.10-13); bride sheltering in the atoning sacrifice (v.14); bridegroom turns her eyes to Calvary; her search for him (3:1-3), help of watchmen (v.3) and her reward in finding him (v.4).

## (3) 3:6 to 5:1

Differs from the previous sections — bride and bridegroom never absent one from the other. He alone speaks. Here, for first time, bridegroom calls the soul his bride, see v.8 RV. In c. 1 she is only his friend (RV marg. for 'O my Love'). In 2: 14 he calls her 'dove', because of the presence of the holy dove, the Holy Spirit within her. In 4: 8, he calls her 'bride' (v.8, RV).

## (4) 5:2 to 8:4

Begins again with absence of the beloved. Bride sleeps, but is wakened by him; too lazy to get up — upon doing so finds her beloved gone. She tells her grief to friendly daughters of Jerusalem, who ask what about her beloved is different from others. She replies. Asked where he had gone, she suddenly remembers. Then he returns; describes the glory of the bride in language that would not shock refined Eastern taste.

## (5) 8: 5-14

Bride and bridegroom once more together coming up from the wilderness. There is now wilderness no longer, nothing but the land flowing with milk and honey.
The king reminds her of her former lowly position (v.5); the bride bursts forth in marvellous description of true love.

# 23
# The Book of Isaiah

**Key word: Salvation**
**Key verse: 43: 3**
**Theme: Salvation of the nation by Jehovah through judgment and grace**

## For young converts
When the great Augustine asked Ambrose which of the sacred books was best to be studied after his conversion, the answer was 'Isaiah'. Certainly nowhere else in the Old Testament have we so clear a view of the grace of God. This book has been called 'The Gospel according to Isaiah', its writer 'the fifth evangelist', 'the prophet of redemption'. Because of this, and its noble language, rich vocabulary, and style, we venture to think that the advice of Ambrose was excellent.

## The prophet
Isaiah was a man of royal blood, his father, Amoz, being a younger son of Joash, king of Judah. He was, moreover, a man of strong and commanding personality, became a statesman, and wielded a tremendous influence in the State. He married one who shared the prophetical gift, had at least two sons (7: 3; 8: 3, 18) laboured for sixty years, and died a martyr, in the reign of Manasseh, at (tradition states) the age of 120.

## Style
His is one of the most beautiful and sublime of all the prophetic writings. He has been called the greatest of the prophets. With the exception of four chapters (36 to 39), it is all magnificent poetry. It abounds in metaphors, (e.g. 2: 19; 24: 20). For the topical method of Bible study this book provides a rich store of material. For example:

## Topical study
1 There are seven everlasting things in Isaiah: salvation (45: 17); light (60: 19); joy (35: 10); strength (26: 4); kindness (54: 8); covenant (55: 3); and judgment (33: 14).
2 Construct from its pages a life of our Lord: his birth (7: 14; 9: 6), family (11: 1), anointing 11: 2), character (11: 3, 4), plain diet and simplicity of life (7: 15), gentleness (42: 1-4), death (c. 53), resurrection (25: 8), and glorious reign (11: 3-16, c. 33 etc.).
3 Note its teaching concerning the Holy Spirit (10: 27; 11: 2; 32: 15; 40: 7, 13; 42: 1; 44: 3; 59: 19, 21; 61: 1; 63: 10).
4 Search for its teaching concerning comfort (40: 1; 51: 3, 12; 66: 13; 61: 2, 3, 12; 63: 9; also 43: 1, 2; 50: 10).
5 Also note (a) Its hint concerning the Trinity ('Us' 6: 8). (b) The marginal rendering of 26: 4, and 59: 15. (c) Its prophecy concerning the end of war (2: 4; 11: 9; 14: 7). (d) Its three 'Blesseds' (30: 18; 32: 20; 56: 2). (e) Lord as king of Israel (6: 5; 44: 6, and 43: 15). (f) Remnant of Israel to be saved (1: 25-27; 2: 2, 3; 6: 13; 11: 11; 18: 7; 27: 12, 13), etc.

## Key words and Message
1 *The Holy One of Israel* is a phrase prominent in this book. It is only found in three Psalms (71, 78, 79), twice in Jeremiah (cc. 50, 51), and in 2 Kings 19: 22, where Isaiah is the speaker. This phrase, and 'Holy One', are met with quite thirty-three times. Evidently the vision he saw when he heard the seraphim crying 'Holy, Holy, Holy' had impressed him, and he could think of the Lord only as the Holy One.
2 Another word prominent in this book is the word 'Salvation'. In no other book of the Old Testament, except in the Psalms, is this word so frequently found. Isaiah's own name means 'Salvation is of Jehovah'. This is the book's message.

## Analysis
This book falls naturally into three parts. Part I begins with the Lord giving the reason for impending judgment and captivity of Israel, but ends with the blessing and regathering of Israel. Part II gives the Lord's intervention and deliverance of Israel. Part III is in three sections, two of which end with the refrain 'There is no peace saith my God to the wicked', and the third with the death of the wicked. Part I begins with a Vision (c. 6); Part III begins with a Voice (c. 40). Part III begins and ends like the New Testament (i.e. with John the Baptist in the wilderness, and a new heaven). Notice also that interspersed with threats and announcements of judgment are cheering promises of blessing, and assurances of a glorious restoration.

## DENUNCIATORY

**The Holy One of Israel provoked, rebuking, and judging**
**(cc. 1 to 35; key 1: 4; 5: 24; 31: 1)**

1 Concerning JUDAH, JERUSALEM (cc. 1 to 12). Degradation of people, call of Isaiah, and Immanuel the divine child, Israel's only hope.
2 Concerning SURROUNDING NATIONS (cc. 13 to 23). Babylon, Moab, Damascus, Egypt, Tyre.
3 Concerning the WORLD (cc. 24 to 35). A remarkable section, largely future.

## HISTORICAL

**The Holy One of Israel delivering**
**(cc. 36 to 39; key 37: 23)**
HEZEKIAH'S TROUBLE (c. 36); PRAYER and DELIVERANCE (c. 37); SICKNESS (c. 38); and FOLLY (c. 39).

## CONSOLATORY

**The Holy One of Israel comforting, redeeming, enriching**
**(cc. 40 to 66; key 40: 1; 43: 3, 14; 49: 7; 53: 3; 60: 17)**

Section One: dominant note 'comfort' (cc. 40 to 48);
Section Two: dominant note 'suffering servant' (cc. 49 to 57). (C. 53 is the central one);
Section Three: dominant theme is 'future glory' (cc. 58 to 66).

# 24
# The Book of Jeremiah

**Key words: Backsliding, Return, Amend, Loved**
**Key verses: 3: 12, 22; 31: 3**
**Theme: The certainty of God's judgment because of sin, yet the tenderness and eternity of the love of God**

## Some glowing opinions
'This book stands to this day second only to the Psalms as the most spiritual book in the Old Testament,' is the testimony of that great Scottish divine, Principal Whyte. 'So far as we have data for judgment, Jeremiah was the healthiest, youngest, bravest, grandest man of Old Testament history,' wrote Dr W. W. White. Isaac Williams says: 'There is nothing in all scripture so eloquent of love and sorrow and consolation as chapters 31, 33 of Jeremiah. No words can be found in any language of such touching beauty.' Surely such eulogies must come as a shock to those who have not seen any beauty in Jeremiah!

## The life of Jeremiah
Unlike many of the prophets, Jeremiah has much to say concerning himself. He was a priest by birth, called to the prophetic ministry at an early age. Pleading his youth (only twenty-one), inexperience, and deficiency of speech, as reasons for not responding to the call, he was assured that Jehovah ordained him to this work before his birth; he then received the divine enduement and commission (1: 1-10). He was commanded not to marry (c. 16). The message he had to bear was stern and solemn, and cost this tender-hearted and truly patriotic man of God much sorrow. His ministry was not acceptable: his own family (12: 6) and his own townsmen (11: 18-23) conspired against him. The people of Jerusalem also conspired against him (18: 18), and eventually beat him and put him in the stocks (20: 1-3). Released, he was assaulted and nearly lost his life (c. 26). He suffered imprisonment several times (37: 11-15; c. 38). On the fall of Jerusalem he was released by Nebuchadnezzar and assisted the new governor, but on the assassination of the latter by Gedaliah, Jeremiah was compelled against his will to accompany the refugees to Egypt. Here he met his death by stoning, after a ministry of forty years.

## Jeremiah's character
He was not 'a man mighty as Elijah, eloquent as Isaiah, or seraphic as Ezekiel, but one who was timid and shrinking, conscious of his helplessness, yearning for a sympathy and love he was never to know — such was the chosen organ through which the word of the Lord came to that corrupt and degenerate age'. Why the selection of such a man for so stern a mission? Because it takes a tender-hearted individual to deliver with force and pathos a stern message of judgment. Tone is important: Jeremiah was the prophet of the broken-heart.

## Some unique contributions
This book, alone of all Bible books, declares (1) that the ark will have no place in restored Israel (3: 16). (2) 'Rising up early and speaking' is a phrase found only in Jeremiah (eleven times, 7: 13, etc.) with the exception of 2 Chronicles 36: 15, which Ezra the Scribe probably borrowed from Jeremiah. (3) It contains the unique phrases 'the generation of his wrath' (7: 19); and 'neither could they blush' — they had lost the power, so shameless was their sin (8: 12). Also note his prayers (1: 6; 4: 10; 12: 1-4; 14: 7, 8, 11, 21; c. 15; 17: 13-18; 18: 19-23; 20: 7; 32: 16-25).

## Texts for preachers
Forsaking a fountain for a broken cistern (2: 13). Insufficiency of mere reformation (2: 22). False and unskilful personal dealing (6: 14). Old paths the best (6: 16). Lost opportunities (8: 20). What to glory in (9: 24). Need of regeneration (13: 23). The Lord a stranger (14: 8). Premature decay (15: 9). The Word of God (15: 16; 23: 29). Condition of heart by nature (17: 9). Second chance here (18: 4). Righteousness personified (23: 6). See also other important truths in 24: 7; 31: 16 and 31-34; 33: 3; 49: 11.

## Message
In reading through this book certain words are frequently met — 'Forsake', 'Forsaken' twenty-four times; 'Backslider', 'Backsliding' (with the exception of once in Proverbs, three times in Hosea, only found in Jeremiah) thirteen times; 'Return' forty-seven times. Jeremiah is a book full of messages for backsliders. Judah had forsaken the Lord — Jeremiah uttered warnings of impending judgment, and besought the people to return to the Lord and amend their ways, as Jehovah still loved them tenderly.

## Analysis
The book is a combination of history, biography, prophecy. It is not written in chronological order.

| CALL | JEREMIAH'S MINISTRY | | | | RETROSPECT |
|---|---|---|---|---|---|
| **Jeremiah's call & commission (c. 1)** Introduction (vv.1-3), call (vv.4-8), enduement (vv.9, 10), and encouragement (vv.11-19). | **(1) In Judah, before the fall of Jerusalem (cc. 2 to 38)** Taking the usual formula of Prophetic utterance: 'The word of the Lord came' as a guide, there appear to be 51 distinct prophecies in this book. | **(2) The fall of Jerusalem (c. 39)** Some particulars of the fall of the city. | **(3) To the remnant in the land after the fall of Jerusalem (cc. 40 to 42)** History and prophecy mingled. | **(4) To those in Egypt (cc. 43 to 51)** 1 To Jews (cc. 43 to 45.) 2 To Gentile Nations (cc. 46 to 51.) | **The Captivity of Judah (c. 52)** The Book begins by foretelling judgment, and ends with its fulfilment. |

# 25
# The Lamentations of Jeremiah

**Key phrase: 'Is it nothing to you?'**
**Key verses: 1: 12; 2: 17; 3: 22, 33**
**Themes: 1 The misery that sin brings. 2 The love and compassion of Jehovah for the subjects of his wrath**

## Author and background
1 This book was written by Jeremiah, after the third siege and fall of Jerusalem. In the Greek version it is prefaced with these words: 'And it came to pass, after Israel was taken captive, and Jerusalem made desolate, that Jeremiah sat weeping, and lamented with this lamentation over Jerusalem, and said.' Instead of exulting over the fulfilment of his prophecies he mourned and wept, a fact well worth our notice.

2 On the face of the Hill of Calvary, where our Lord was crucified, is a dark recess known as 'Jeremiah's Grotto', held to be the place where the prophet sat, gazing at the ruined city, and composed this wail of a broken heart. If this is so, how significant that the mourning patriot's tears for the woes of the city should have been shed so near the spot where the rejected Saviour should suffer for the sins of that city, and indeed of the whole world.

3 Jewish patriots chant this book every Friday at the wailing place in Jerusalem, and it is read in every Jewish synagogue on the fast of the ninth day of August, the day set apart to mourn over the five great calamities which have befallen the nation.

## Opinions
Principal Whyte wrote: 'There is nothing like the Lamentations of Jeremiah in the whole world. There has been plenty of sorrow in every age, and in every land, but such another preacher and author, with such a heart for sorrow, has never again been born. Dante comes next to Jeremiah, and we know that Jeremiah was that great exile's favourite prophet.' We could quote the opinions of others, but this is sufficient.

## A greater than Jeremiah here
There is no doubt that we have a greater than Jeremiah here. Dr Scofield suggestively remarks: 'The touching significance of this book lies in the fact that it is the disclosure of the love and sorrow of Jehovah for the very people whom he is chastening — a sorrow wrought by the Spirit in the heart of Jeremiah.' This book foreshadowed the wailing of the Lord Jesus over the approaching desolation of the holy city. Many passages are charged with messianic meaning (1: 12; 2: 15; 3: 14, 15, 19, 30).

## Style
Each lament is arranged in acrostic form, which is necessarily obscured in our translation. 'Each chapter in Lamentations contains twenty-two verses, and each verse begins with one of the twenty-two letters of the Hebrew alphabet in order, except Chapter 3, which has sixty-six verses, three commencing with A, three with B, and so on; the last chapter is a little irregular.' It is thought that this acrostic method was adopted as an aid to memory.

## Analysis
There are five poems, indicated by the chapters. In each poem, except the last, there are references to the sad ruined condition of the city, followed by a justification of God in dealing so sternly and drastically with his people, and a reference to passers by. Each poem ends with a prayer to the Lord, with the exception of the fourth, but this is made up by the last, which is all prayer. The gem of the whole book is 3: 22, 23.

## FIRST POEM

**The city represented as a weeping widow mourning in solitude**
**(c. 1)**
Jerusalem graphically represented as a widow bereft of her children, sitting alone in the night, weeping. Note characteristic utterances: 'None to comfort' (vv.2, 9, 17, 21), and 'No rest' (v.3), 'No pasture' (v.6), 'No comforter' (v.9).
1 The city in her calamity (vv.1-7)
2 Judgments — God justified (vv.8-11, 18)
3 Passers by — appeal for sympathy (vv.12-19)
4 Prayer — appeal to the Lord (vv.20-22)

## SECOND POEM

**The city represented as a veiled woman now mourning amidst the ruins**
**(c. 2)**
A vivid description of the siege of Jerusalem. The prophet dwells principally on God, author and inflicter of these sore punishments.
1 The city — siege and ruin (vv.1-14)
2 Passers by — their scorn and cruel taunts (vv.15, 16)
3 Judgments foretold (v.17)
4 Prayer — to the Lord (v.18-22)

## THIRD POEM

**The city represented as, and by, the weeping prophet mourning before Jehovah the Judge**
**(c. 3)**
Considered one of the most remarkable in the Old Testament, this poem differs in that the prophet identifies himself with his people, making their miseries and sorrows his own.
1 City — prophet a man of affliction (vv.1-20) prophet a man of hope (vv.21-36)
2 Judgments — God justified (vv.37-39)
3 Appeal to Nation (vv.40-54)
4 Appeal to the Lord (vv.55-66)

## FOURTH POEM

**The city represented as gold, dimmed, changed, degraded**
**(c. 4)**
1 City — by series of contrasts horrors of the siege are depicted (vv.1-10)
2 Judgments — God justified (vv.11-16)
3 Edom's cruelty (vv.17-20)
4 Retribution on Edom (vv.21, 22)

## FIFTH POEM

**The city represented as a suppliant pleading with the Lord**
**(c. 5)**
There was no closing prayer in the previous poem, but this is one long earnest appeal to Jehovah.
1 City — calamity (vv.1-6)
2 Sin — confession (v.7)
3 Suffering (vv.8-18)
4 Appeal to the Lord (vv.19-22)

# 26
# The Book of Ezekiel

**Key phrase: The glory of the Lord**
**Key verses: 1: 28; 10: 4, 18; 43: 2**
**Theme: The goodness and severity of God**

## Ezekiel
Ezekiel was a priest belonging to the aristocracy of Jerusalem (1: 1-3) and, at the age of twenty-five, just eleven years before the destruction of the Temple, was carried captive to Babylon. He was contemporary with Jeremiah and Daniel. In Babylon he dwelt in his own house (8: 1). He was married, but his wife died in the year when the final siege of Jerusalem began (24: 18). He began his ministry five years after reaching Babylon, at the age of thirty, when Jeremiah was approaching the end of his great and tragic career.

## His mission
By false prophets the captives were led to imagine that Jerusalem would not be destroyed, and they would soon be restored to their beloved city and land. Jeremiah heard of this, and from Jerusalem wrote them a letter (Jer. c. 29). Ezekiel began his ministry the following year, endorsing all that Jeremiah had said, and endeavouring to convince them that before they could ever hope to return to Jerusalem they must return to their Lord. Though the task was a difficult one, and though at first he met with very great opposition, ultimately he was blessed with success, and his people's return to their Lord and their land was largely the fruit of his ministry.

## Prophet of the Spirit
Each of the three great prophets emphasized one person in the blessed Trinity. Ezekiel is the prophet of the Spirit, as Isaiah is the prophet of the Son, and Jeremiah the prophet of the Father. The ministry of the Spirit is most noticeable in this book — there are at least twenty-five references to the Spirit. See 2: 2; 3: 12, 14, 24, etc. His name means 'whom God strengthens', and the agent in his strengthening was the Holy Spirit.

## Notable truths
(1) Ezekiel speaks of Israel in Egypt more than any other prophet. It is only in this book (20: 1-9) that we learn of Israel's idolatry in Egypt, and of God's thought to destroy them there because of it. How near they were to destruction! But God can do for his own name's sake what he cannot possibly do for ours, and he spared them. (2) It is in this book alone that we learn of satan's past history (28: 11-19). Here we get a glimpse into the history of our great adversary. (3) It is here only that we have very full details of the Temple yet to be built (cc. 40 to 42), and of the new river (c. 47).

## Analysis
1 This is a book many do not care to read. One reason is, they do not understand its key, structure, and message.
2 Its key phrase is 'the glory of the Lord', which occurs fourteen times in the first eleven chapters. In the Old Testament 'the glory of the Lord' means the visible light which shone between the cherubim in the Most Holy Place in Tabernacle and Temple proclaiming the presence of God. Before the destruction of the Temple, Ezekiel in vision saw the glory of the Lord leave the Temple. There is in 9: 3 a brief statement of this fact, further particulars being given in c. 10. As he looked he saw above the ark and cherubim the likeness of God's throne, which had wheels, and was therefore a kind of royal chariot (10: 1). Then the glory of the Lord removed to the threshold of the house (10: 4), then from off the threshold and stood at the door of the east gate (10: 18, 19), then from the Temple and city to Olivet (11: 22, 23). Thus slowly, reluctantly, majestically, the glory of the Lord left the sanctuary and the city. But the glory has yet to return (c. 43). Ezekiel's ministry began with a vision of God, and it closes with a vision of God among his people. His message is the severity of God to his backslidden and unrepentant people, and his goodness to the penitent.

---

| Preparation and call of the prophet | Prophecies of destruction of Jerusalem | | Prophecies against seven nations | Prophecies in relation to Israel's future | |
|---|---|---|---|---|---|
| **The Appearance** of the glory of the Lord (cc. 1 to 3) | **The Departure** of the glory of the Lord (cc. 4 to 24) | (9) False prophetesses (c. 13); (10) Various parables, with other important teaching, calculated to lead to reformation and repentance (cc. 14 to 24). | **God's Glory** and the surrounding peoples (cc. 25 to 32) | **The Return** of the glory of the Lord (cc. 33 to 48) | (9) Division of Jerusalem (cc. 45, 46); (10) Life-giving waters (c. 47); (11) Division of the land (c. 48). (Many consider this the richest portion of the whole book.) |
| The appearance of the glory and the result in the prophet's life. 1 Opened heavens and a vision of God the Son as man on the Throne (c. 1) 2 The workers' commission (c. 2) food (3: 1-3) task (3: 4-11) enduement (3: 12-14) duties (3: 15-21) 3 The appearance of the glory of the Lord (3: 22-27). | **Reasons of departure of glory of God.** Ezekiel begins his ministry to Israel: (1) Siege of Jerusalem foretold (c. 4); (2) Horrors of the siege (c. 5); (3) A remnant to be preserved (c. 6); (4) Its awful desolation (c. 7); (5) Idolatry in high circles of society (c. 8); (6) Remnant marked for preservation (c. 9); (7) **Departure of the glory** (cc. 10, 11); (8) Punishment delayed but certain (c. 12); | | **God of glory acting in defence of his people.** Seven prophecies uttered in the interval between the knowledge of Nebuchadnezzar's siege (24: 2), and news that Jerusalem was taken (33: 21). Observe, God was against these heathen nations, not only because of idolatry, but because of their ill-treatment of Israel — Ammon, Moab, Edom, Philistines (c. 25, see c. 35); Tyre (cc. 26 to 28); Egypt (cc. 29 to 32). | **Preparation for return of the glory of Lord**, given after a 3 years' silence. (1) Promise of restoration to the penitents (c. 33); (2) The Good Shepherd (c. 34); (3) Gospel according to Ezekiel (c. 36); (4) Great national revival depicted (c. 37); (5) Israel's future enemies vanquished (cc. 38, 39); (6) The New Sanctuary yet to be erected (cc. 40 to 42); (7) **Return of the glory of God** (c. 43); (8) The mysterious prince (c. 44); | |

# 27
# The Book of Daniel

Key phrase: 'The most high ruleth'
Key verses: 2: 22; 4: 25
Theme: The universal sovereignty of God

**Daniel**
1 Daniel, like Ezekiel, was among the captives carried to Babylon on the occasion of Nebuchadnezzar's invasion of Palestine (1: 1-3).

2 It is believed that he belonged to a family of high rank, if not of the royal house, and that he was taken to Babylon at the age of sixteen, eight years before Ezekiel. If that is so, then Daniel was among the number captured in the first invasion, in the third year of Jehoiakim, while Ezekiel was taken in the second invasion.
3 His whole life from that time was spent in Babylon (see 1: 21, a period of sixty-nine years). In a vile court he lived so saintly a life that in Ezekiel 14: 14-20 and 28: 3 he is referred to as a pattern or model of righteousness.
4 Though belonging to a captive race, and never swerving in his devotion and loyalty to Jehovah, he rose to the highest position in the State, and exercised his own powerful political ministry in three kingdoms, those of Babylon, Media, and Persia.

**Prophet**
He was not only a public State servant, but he was also a prophet of God. His prophecies — which deal more fully with Gentile nations than with his own Jewish nation — are among the most remarkable in the whole of the Bible.

**Lord's imprimatur**
In Matthew 24: 15 our Lord set his seal upon this book as inspired of God. Our Lord's own title 'Son of man' is based on 7: 13.

**Message**
It has several messages. The Lord's loyal and obedient servants (1) often are blessed with worldly success (1: 9, 20; 2: 48, 49) and (2) are trusted with his secrets (2: 19, 22, 47); (3) in times of suffering and trial they have the comfort of his presence (3: 25). (4) It also sounds a loud warning against pride (4: 30-37); (5) and not honouring and glorifying God (5: 22, 23). But its chief message is its proclamation of the universal sovereignty of God (4: 25).

**Analysis**
It is in two main divisions — the first dealing chiefly with historic events, the second with visions and then with interpretations. Daniel's name means either 'God my judge' (suggesting God's defence of him), or 'Judge of God', i.e. one who delivers judgment in the name of the Lord; it suggests six minor divisions as follows:

---

## HISTORICAL (Written in the 3rd person)

### HEATHEN
## Customs
**judged**
**(c. 1)**
1 Though Daniel was dedicated to Baal, (his new name indicates 'favourite of Baal'), he remained true to Jehovah.
2 The palace food — meat killed with blood, and offered to idols — he and his companions refused.
3 God blessed him and his companions for their loyalty, and gave them success.

### HEATHEN
## Philosophy
**judged**
**(c. 2)**
1 Heathen philosophers failed to tell dream.
2 The interpretation of this dream gives the course and end of Gentile world dominion, from Daniel's day to end of this age.
3 Note the stone (2: 34, 35) does not grow until it has broken into pieces the great image. It is after this total destruction of Gentile dominion that God's kingdom is set up.

### HEATHEN
## Pride
**judged**
**(cc. 3, 4)**
1 The erection of this great image was Nebuchadnezzar's attempt to unify the religions of his empire by self-deification.
2 This attempt will be repeated by the Beast, the last head of the Gentile world-dominion (Rev. 13: 11-15; 19: 20).
3 Note the significance of the rise of the present day religion of Humanism.

### HEATHEN
## Impiety
**judged**
**(c. 5)**
1 By death of Belshazzar.
2 From inscriptions found and deciphered, we know now that Belshazzar and his father Nabonidus ruled jointly over Babylon and the Empire.
3 That while Belshazzar fell in the capture of the imperial city, his father surrendered at Borsippa.

### HEATHEN
## Persecutors
**judged**
**(c. 6)**
1 Daniel must have been about 80 years old when this trial befell him.
2 Daniel put 'God first', and the Lord defended him.
3 See how God was glorified by the loyalty of his servant.

---

## PROPHETICAL (Written in 1st person)

## The Nations of the World
**judged; the establishment of the everlasting kingdom**
**(7: 1 to 12: 13)**

**1 Vision of Beasts (c. 7)**
In c. 2 the world kingdoms are seen by the heathen king in *outward* unity and glory, yet without life, a metal colossus. Here they appear to the prophet in their real character, instinct with *beast-life*, **terrible** animal power.
**2 Vision of Ram and Goat (c. 8)**
Further particulars concerning the Medo-Persian and Macedonian kingdoms (vv.5-8 so impressed Alexander the Great that he preserved Israel).

**3 Vision of the Seventy weeks (c. 9)**
A most remarkable chapter. (The 70 weeks are 70 periods of 7 years.)
**4 Vision of the Lord (c. 10)**
In vv.1-9 and 16-21 the vision of the Lord; in vv.10-15 an angel appears.
**5 Further prophecies concerning Daniel's time and to the end of time (11: 1 to 12: 3)**
**6 Closing words (12: 4-13)**

# 28
# The Book of Hosea

**Key word: Return (15 times)**
**Key verse: 14: 1**
**Theme: An exhibition of God's method in the restoration of backsliders**

## The prophet
1 Hosea, contemporary with Amos, Isaiah, and Micah, laboured in Samaria, though in his later years, having long appealed to his doomed countrymen in vain, he retired to Judea. It is believed that the latter portions of this book were written in Judea.
2 He was spared many years to labour for his Lord. From 1: 1, we judge that his ministry was exercised seventy-two years. It has been calculated that if he began his prophetic ministry at the age of twenty, he would die at an age between 92 and 98.
3 He had a very sad domestic trial — the unfaithfulness of his wife — and God spoke to Israel through that lamentable trouble. This is the pivot of the whole book.

## His mission
Hosea's message was principally to Israel (i.e. the ten tribes). The name Ephraim occurs in this book over thirty-five times, and the name Israel with equal frequency, while Judea is not mentioned more than fourteen times, and Jerusalem is never mentioned.

## Character
1 Hosea's writings are more poetical than most of the prophets — they abound in striking metaphors.
2 The attribute of God most in Hosea's thoughts is 'Lord'. The aspect of the divine character on which Hosea dwells most fondly is that of husband and wife. (Israel is Jehovah's bride, while the Church is the Lamb's bride.)

## Analysis
1 Some consider Hosea to be the most difficult of all the prophetic books. It is certainly not an easy one to study.
2 At first sight there does not seem to be any order in it, but after much study one sees beautiful order.
3 It is in reality a clear treatise on repentance for backsliders. Here we have a delightful exhibition of God's methods in the restoration of a backslidden people.

## Israel's ignoble condition
**when selected by God**
**(c. 1)**
1 Hosea's marriage with an abandoned woman (v.2). (Calvin and others think it a parable: there is no reason for not taking it to be fact.)
2 Birth of two sons and a daughter, significant names being given (vv.4-9).
3 The marriage was to teach Israel, (and every believer) that they were not selected by God because of worthiness in themselves; they were as unworthy of honourable marriage as Gomer.
4 In v.2 Hosea shows Israel's troubles began by departing from God. See how he ends (14: 1).

## Israel's awful fall
**(c. 2)**
1 The unfaithfulness of Hosea's wife a picture of Israel's unfaithfulness (vv.1-5).
2 Chastisement (vv.6-13).
3 V.14 with 8: 13 seems to suggest Israel has to have another Egyptian and wilderness experience.
4 To end with Israel restored to the Lord for ever (v.19).
Note. By God's blessing valleys of Achor (trouble) become doors of blessing places for song (v.15).

## Israel's ransom price paid
**(c. 3)**
1 Though the prophet's wife has deserted him he is still to love her (v.1).
2 He enters into agreement by which provision is made for her (v.2) on certain conditions.
3 It does not seem that they were to live together yet: — fulfilled in Israel today. Not living as Jehovah's wife, but living a separate life (vv.4, 5).
4 Evidently David has again to reign over Israel (v.5).

## The terrible results of Israel's fall
**pointed out by the Lord**
**(cc. 4, 5)**
1 No morality (vv.1-5).
2 Wilful ignorance (vv.6-11) and idolatry (vv.12-19).
3 But the crowning calamity, the hiding of the face of the Lord (See 5: 15). (Compare 4: 7 with 14: 8, a powerful gospel lesson. The first gives a picture of a nation hugging its idols, the second, of the same nation throwing them away. 'I have heard him' is the secret.)

## Israel's penitent cry
**(6: 1-3)**
1 The decision of the remnant in the last days.
2 Note the force of v.3. To unrepentant Israel, he is 'a lion' (5: 14), but to repentant ones the gentle, fertilizing shower.
3 If our goodness proceeds from God, it will not be as the 'morning cloud' or 'early dew' (v.4).

## The Lord probes Israel's wounds
**before applying the healing balsam**
**(6: 4 to 13: 16)**
1 To make sure Israel is thoroughly repentant the Lord probes their wounds to test and deepen their penitence.
2 Note the metaphors used to describe the character and condition of Israel (6: 4; 7: 4, 8, 11, 12; 8: 7, 9; 10: 1, 11, 12; 12: 1).
3 Note the pathos of 11: 8.

## The prophet's final appeal to Israel
**(14: 1-3)**
1 Confess their sad state entirely due to own sin;
2 Repudiate all hope of help in man . . .
3 . . . with every sign of genuine repentance. Note. How comforting last clause of v.3 is for fatherless.

**The Lord's gracious reply**
## Israel's final restoration
**(14: 4-9)**
(1) Healing (v.4), (2) Loved by Lord (v.4), (3) Refreshed by Lord (v.5), (4) Growing (v.5). (5) Beauty (v.6), (6) Fragrance (v.6), (7) Fruitfulness (v.6), (8) Companionship of Lord (v.7).
1 Note magnificent conclusion (v.9).
2 Healing their backsliding means more than forgiving the backslider — it means that Jehovah will remove the cause.

# 29
# The Book of Joel

Key phrase: 'The day of the Lord'
Key verse: 2: 28, 29
Theme: The value and importance of repentance

## Joel
1 Nothing is known of the prophet Joel beyond the short introduction he gives in 1: 1.
2 The first one to bear that name in scripture was Samuel's elder son (1 Sam. 8: 2), and it means 'Jehovah is my God'.
3 Probably he was the very earliest of the prophetic writers, exercising his ministry in Judah in the early reign of Joash (2 Kgs cc. 11, 12). He would in his youth have known both Elijah and Elisha.

## Notable
1 Competent literary authorities declare that, from standpoint of style, this small book is a literary gem. Its 'style is pre-eminently pure, and is characterised by smoothness and fluency, strength and tenderness'.
2 But it is specially notable for three things. (a) It contains the grandest description in all literature of locust devastation. (b) It gives the first intimation of the outpouring of the Spirit upon all flesh (2: 28, 29); and (c) its prophecies are remarkable for their scope, extending from Joel's day to the end of time.

## Occasion
1 There had been a very severe visitation of drought, and a plague of locusts, spreading ruin on every hand.
2 Though Moses (Deut. 28: 38, 39), and Solomon (1 Kgs 8: 37) had mentioned locusts as one of the instruments of divine chastisement, the people in this instance had not recognised them as such.

3 Joel's mission was to point out the sad condition of the national spiritual life as the reason why the plague was sent, and to exhort to national repentance as the essential step in returning to God.

## Prophetic
1 But Joel also pointed out that the invasion of locusts was only a type of another more terrible invasion.
2 No doubt this prophecy had a partial fulfilment in the swarms of heathen who invaded the land in those days.
3 But there are details which have never yet had a fulfilment, and are yet future, for the last days.

## Key
1 The key to the understanding of the book is the phrase 'The day of the Lord' (1: 15; 2: 1, 11, 31; 3: 14).
2 'The day of the Lord' 'will commence with the removal of the church. It is the day when the Lord will judge and interfere once more directly in the course of this world's politics. It lasts for a thousand years.'

## Message, Analysis
Joel has been called 'the prophet of Religious revival'. He saw that genuine repentance lay at the foundation of all real revival, and this he laboured to produce. This is a book of repentance. The rent heart followed by rent veil, and rent heaven (see analysis (5) 3) signifies that access to God and pentecostal blessing follow true repentance.

| 1 The national calamity described and interpreted (1: 1-14, 16-20) | 2 The day of the Lord foreshadowed (1: 15) | 3 The day of the Lord foretold (2: 1-10; 3: 9-15) | 4 Intervention for Israel by the Lord (2: 11; 3: 16) | 5 This the reason why Israel should repent (2: 12-17) | 6 The Lord's glorious response to Israel's repentance (2: 18-29; 3: 1-8, 17-21) |
|---|---|---|---|---|---|
| 1 The unparalleled calamity (vv.1-3) | The prophet sees in this attack of locusts an emblem of a more terrible attack by swarms of heathen soldiers in his day, but more particularly in the last days yet to come. | 1 Number of, and injury done, by enemies (2: 1-10) | 1 The Lord's sudden and swift intervention to save Israel from annihilation. | 1 Note 'Therefore'. | 1 Blessing (2: 18, 19) |
| 2 Desolation described (vv.4-13) | | 2 Lord's challenge to Israel's enemies (3: 9-15) | 2 3: 16 'Hope of his people' is in RV 'a refuge unto' and in marg. of AV/KJV 'a place of repair' or 'harbour'. | 2 The Lord's voluntary intervention is the real reason why Israel should repent and turn to the Lord. | 2 Emancipation (2: 20) |
| 3 National fast urged (v.14) | | 3 Promise of preservation of a remnant (2: 30-32). | | 3 A rent heart (v.13) is followed by a rent veil (Matt. 27: 51) and rent heaven (Isa. 64: 1). | 3 Prosperity (2: 21-27) |
| 4 The mourning of the prophet (vv.16-20) | | | | | 4 Outpouring of Spirit (2: 28-29) |
| | | | | | 5 Judgment of Gentile nations (3: 1-8) |
| | | | | | 6 Full kingdom blessing (3: 17-21) |

# 30
# The Book of Amos

**Key word: Punishment**
**Key verse: 4: 12**
**Theme: National sin means national judgment**

## The prophet
1 Amos was a native of Tekoa, a place twelve miles from Jerusalem, and six from Bethlehem. He therefore belonged to Judah.
2 He was not a courtier like Isaiah, or a priest like Jeremiah, but an ordinary working man. He was a herdsman, and a 'dresser' (1: 1 RV) of sycamore trees. 'Dresser' means 'nipper' or 'pincher' — the sycamore fruit (the wild fig eaten only by the poorest) can only be ripened by puncturing it.
3 He was contemporary with Hosea and Jonah. Though a native of Judah he prophesied in and against Israel.

## The time
1 'Two years before the earthquake' (1: 1), he commenced his prophetic ministry at Bethel. Amos foretold this earthquake (5: 8; 6: 11; 8: 8; 9: 5, RV).
2 This earthquake must have been of exceptional severity, for Zechariah speaks of it nearly 300 years later as an event well remembered (Zech. 14: 5).

## A model worker
Incidentally this book provides us with a treatise on preaching, and portrays Amos as a model worker for God. Note:
1 *His humility.* He makes no attempt to hide the bare facts of his past life and employment; he was not ashamed to make known his lowly birth and occupation. There was in him an entire absence of 'side'. His exaltation to prophetic rank did not spoil him.
2 *His industry.* Owing to his trade he often lived a solitary life, yet he spent it in communion with God, and in close observation of nature. The illustrations scattered through this book are all drawn from his every-day life, proving his keenness of sight and originality of mind.
3 *His wisdom.* He did not preach over the heads of the people, but employed terms quite familiar to all of them.
4 *His astuteness.* He caught the attention of the people right away by speaking first against their enemies.
5 *His faithfulness.* he was not a tickler of the popular ear, but dealt faithfully with the people, making straight tracks for their consciences.
6 *His steadfastness.* He refused to be turned from the work God had given him (7: 10-17). He kept his eye on his divine master.
7 *His message.* He had a 'Thus saith the Lord', a message direct from God. It was a timely one, too, suitable to that God-forsaking age.
8 *His success.* He was blessed with wonderful success (7: 10). He wielded an influence over the whole land.

## Message
Amos' burden was one concerning punishment. He had a stern message for that luxurious and self-indulgent age. He was the prophet of woe. The book shows that national sin means national judgment, and while the sin of individuals will be judged at the Great White Throne, nations are judged in this world and within time. The history of the world proves this.

## Analysis
A great Bible teacher divides this book into four sections; it also falls into five sections, both arrangements shown as follows:

| DECLAMATION | PROCLAMATION | | REVELATION | RESTORATION |
|---|---|---|---|---|
| **Punishment of surrounding nations (1: 2 to 2: 3)** | **1 Punishment of Judah and Israel (2: 4-16)** | **2 Three discourses against Israel (3: 1 to 6: 9)** | **Visions concerning Israel (7: 1 to 9: 10)** | **Restoration of all Israel (9: 11-15)** |
| 1 Prophecies against surrounding nations, occupying territory given to Israel by God. | 1 The thunder-storm of God's wrath rolls over all surrounding kingdoms, touches Judah (vv.4, 5) and at length falls with crashing effect upon Israel. | 1 Each begins with 'Hear'. 2 Address to Israel, and 'whole family', *i.e.* Judah. | 1 Visions: grasshoppers (7: 1); fire (7: 4); plumb-line (7: 7); summer fruit (8: 1); the Lord 'standing on the altar' (9: 1). | Here is foretold the Lord's return and the establishment of the Davidic Kingdom — restoration (v.11), possession (v.12), prosperity (vv.13, 14), perpetuity (v.15). |
| 2 Though sent expressly to Israel, opens his ministry announcing coming judgment on six heathen nations — To gain the attention of Israel, To show Israel that God is no respecter of persons when sin is concerned. | 2 Note charges God was compelled to lay at their door (2: 4, 6, 7, 8 etc.) | 3 In 4: 2, he rudely dispels fond idea Israel hugged in national pride, that to the favoured nation no harm could happen. 4 In chapter 5, a discourse on 'seeking the Lord'. | Notable verses: 7: 1 'After king's mowings' — let God have his part. 8: 11; 7: 13 (the only time 'chapel' is mentioned in the Bible). | Notable verse: 9: 15. |
| Notable verses: Quaint expression in 1: 3 etc., 'For three transgressions . . .' | Notable verse: 2: 13 — God burdened with sins as waggon with sheaves. | Notable verses: 4: 12; 3: 3; 6: 1. | | |

# 31
# The Book of Obadiah

Key word: Retribution
Key verse: v.15
Theme: Solemn warning against the perils of pride and anti-semitism

## Obadiah
Absolutely nothing is known of the writer of this book. Several Obadiahs are mentioned in the Old Testament, but there is nothing to indicate that either of them wrote this book. His name means 'the Servant (or Worshipper) of Jehovah'. It is difficult to fix the time when the book was written, but verses 10-14 clearly prove that it must have been written after the fall of Jerusalem (2 Chron. 36: 17-21).

## Purpose
This is the shortest book in the Old Testament. It is a brilliant prophetic cameo. It forms a sharp manifesto against the fierce Idumeans, who were the perpetual enemies of Israel. It gives the character, career, doom, and downfall of Edom.

## History
The Edomites, or Idumeans, were the descendants of Esau. They were a proud, bitter, resentful people, ever seeking opportunity to harm Jacob's descendants. Governed at first by dukes, and afterward by kings (Gen. c. 36), they were in their golden age when Israel was led out of Egyptian bondage. Israel and Edom were perpetually at war. When Nebuchadnezzar captured Jerusalem, Edom rejoiced over Israel's downfall, and cruelly took part in the plundering and massacre (see Psa. 137: 7). In days gone by, God had commanded his people to treat Edom kindly (Deut. 23: 7), but now their atrocious conduct had filled up their cup of iniquity, and sentence of condemnation and annihilation was passed upon them. After Israel's restoration, Cyrus, king of Persia, overcame them, slaughtering thousands of them. They suffered another crushing defeat by the Jews, under the Maccabees, and slowly disappeared as a nation until their very name perished.

## Gospel
What a gospel gem is here in vv.17, 18! This gives the preliminaries to victory: delivered, sanctified, and enriched, we shall be able to live the all-victorious life.

## Message and Analysis
This brief book has a two-fold message — a warning against sinful pride and godless defiance (v.3), and against hating and harming the Jews, whose cause God himself will undertake, and whose enemies he will destroy.

---

### 1 Edom's
## Humiliation
**(vv.1-9)**
Note the steps in Edom's humiliation:
1 The Lord at work influencing the nations (RV for 'heathen') against Edom (v.1);
2 In consequence, the small nation of Edom was 'despised' (v.2);
3 They would be dragged out of their apparently impregnable refuges (vv.3, 4);
4 They would be despoiled, but not as by thieves (vv.5, 6);
5 Neighbouring nations with whom they had entered into covenant, would break their agreements and rend them (v.7);
6 Even the noted wisdom of their counsellors (v.8), and the strength and courage of their soldiers, would be taken away, and would fail them.

### 2 Edom's
## Crime
**(vv.10-14)**
Note the telling description of Edom's sins:
1 'Violence against thy brother Jacob' (v.10);
2 Refused help ('stoodest on the other side'), and acted as the conquerors (v.11);
3 They rejoiced at Jacob's discomfiture and jeered at them (v.12);
4 They also took a share in looting (v.13);
5 And, worse than all, hunted the fugitives and handed them over to the enemy (v.14).

### 3 Edom's
## Doom
**(vv.15-21)**
At first sight this section seems to deal exclusively with Judah's glorious restoration, but on closer scrutiny it is seen to be introduced only to show how and when Edom's destruction was to be brought about.
1 Verdict announced (vv.10, 15).
2 Israel would be delivered, sanctified, and enriched (v.17), and after this would be an instrument in Edom's destruction (v.18), and possess the land of Edom, etc. (vv.19, 20).
3 This came to pass in the time of the Maccabees — though vv.19-21 have yet a more glorious fulfilment.
4 What a glorious finish: 'The kingdom shall be the Lord's.'

# 32
# The Book of Jonah

**Key phrase:** 'For I knew'
**Key verse:** 4: 2
**Theme:** God, the God of the Gentile as well as of the Jew

## Literary value
That eminent literary authority Charles Reade, declared that the book of Jonah is the most beautiful story ever written in so small a compass. It is a perfect gem, and simply full of teaching.

## History
This book forms one of the battle-grounds of modern destructive criticism. By many it is considered to be only an allegory, with no historical background whatever. But 2 Kings 14: 25, proves Jonah to be a historical personage. Then the historical character of this man is vouched for by our Lord (Matt. 12: 39-41). Therefore we have no hesitation in affirming that here we have fact not fiction; history, not fable.

## The prophet
1 Jonah was of Gath — hepher, near Nazareth, therefore a Galilean, proving that the Pharisees lied when they said 'out of Galilee ariseth no prophet' (John 7: 52). Nahum and Malachi also were of Galilee.
2 He began his prophetic career as Elisha closed his. Some ancient Jewish authorities were of the opinion that Jonah was the widow's son of Zarephath, whom Elijah raised from the dead.
3 A prophecy of his is preserved for us in 2 Kings 14: 25-27. He was therefore a fully accredited prophet.

## Key
4: 2 is the key, giving the clue to the whole book. Why did Jonah disobey the Lord? (1) Not because of cowardice — there is abundant evidence of his courage in this book. (2) Nor was it because he was 'out of sympathy with foreign missions'. (But see Lesson 2 below) (3) Nor was it out of regard for his own personal honour as a prophet. (4) The motive that moved him to disobey God was a false patriotism. Assyria was Israel's great enemy. He wished to leave them to perish in their sins, and thus Israel would be rid of their ancient foe. To go and preach to them might lead to their salvation, and their consequent preservation. This he wanted to avoid: (Nineveh was capital of hated Assyria).

## Lessons
1 It shows how futile are man's efforts to frustrate the divine purposes of grace.
2 Its chief message is the statement found in Romans 3: 29. It was designed to teach God's people that he was the God of the Gentiles as well as of the Jews, that he had purposes of grace and love toward them as well as toward Israel. This lesson Israel never learned in spite of the eloquent teaching of this book.

## Type
1 In Matthew 12: 38-42, Jesus declared that Jonah was a type of his own entombment and resurrection, and the people of Nineveh an example of true genuine repentance.
2 Jonah is typical, not only of the Lord, but of Israel. Dr Bullinger has very suggestively pointed this out. 'Jonah is God's ambassador sent to preach repentance to the Gentiles. So was Israel. He objects to Gentiles being thus blessed, and flees from the unpleasant task. He is visited by a divinely sent storm, and is thrown into the sea. So Israel is now cast into the sea of the nations; but, like Jonah, is not lost, for presently Israel will be cast up on the earth, and become the ambassadors of Jehovah, and the conveyors of blessing to the Gentiles.'

## 1 The prophet's Commission
(1: 1, 2)
1 He must have been an experienced prophet when the call came. The abrupt 'Now' seems to indicate that this was a continuation not a beginning of his ministry.
2 Nineveh was indeed a 'great city', about sixty miles in circumference, covering 216 square miles, with a population of 600,000.

## 2 The prophet's Disobedience
(1: 3-17)
1 The prophet deliberately disobeyed the Lord.
2 'He paid the fare thereof.' We always have to 'pay' when we disobey him.
3 Note the four 'prepared' things in this book (1: 17; 4: 6-8).
4 How like the sleep of the sinner is 1: 6.
5 Salvation through substitution is taught by 1: 15.

## 3 The prophet's Prayer
(c. 2)
1 This was the prayer of one in great trouble, and in a strange place.
2 Note. Its disjointed condition. Its graphic description.

## 4 The prophet Re-commissioned
(3: 1-3)
1 The joy of not being cast off for faithlessness and disobedience!
2 He had to carry the Lord's message: 'the preaching that I bid thee'.
3 The prophet readily obeyed.

## 5 The prophet's Success
(3: 4-10)
1 Jonah was successful because he was a living witness of the truths he proclaimed. Looking upon him they would get a gleam of hope.
2 Note — Nineveh 'believed God' and repented.

## 6 The prophet Reproved
(c. 4)
1 Jonah had a lingering hope that destruction would come to the Assyrians.
2 God gave him an object lesson.
3 Note the abruptness of its finish. 'God's tender accents are the last that reach the ear — the abruptness of the close makes them the more impressive.'

# 33
# The Book of Micah

Key phrase: 'Who is a God like unto thee?'
Key verses: 6: 8; 7: 18
Themes: 1 God's Hatred of injustice. 2 God's Hatred of ritualism 3 God's Delight in pardoning

## Writer

1 Nothing is known of Micah beyond that stated in 1: 1, viz. that he belonged to Judah, was contemporary of Isaiah, and that Isaiah must have been prophesying seventeen or eighteen years before he began his ministry. Though a countryman, his ministry was principally to the cities.

2 His name means 'Who is like Jehovah?' and is an index to his character. To him, God was everything. He had an exalted conception of the holiness, righteousness and compassion of God. He closes his book by exclaiming, 'Who is a God like unto thee?' and he meant what he implied. Judging by his writings, he was a man of wonderful power, of calm, sane judgment, tenderhearted, yet faithful, and for all this he gave God the praise (3: 8).

## Notable

The book is notable for several reasons: (a) It is written in an entrancing style. It is full of poetic beauty, and in consequence is a favourite with students of the minor prophets. (b) It contains a remarkable prophecy concerning Jerusalem (3: 12), (c) and the future glory of Jerusalem (c. 4). (d) It locates the birthplace of the Saviour (5: 2); (e) and, as Dean Stanley says, it contains 'one of the most sublime and impassioned declarations of spiritual religion that the Old Testament contains' (6: 6-8). (f) To crown all, in 7: 18, 19, we

have, as Dr Pierson says: 'a little poem of twelve lines in the Hebrew . . . one of the most exquisite things to be found in the entire Old Testament, (that) would alone be sufficient to prove that this Bible is the Word of God, for there is nothing like it in all the literature of men.'

## Quoted

An author is proud of the day when he is quoted either in print or on the public platform. There are three notable occasions when Micah was quoted: (a) By the elders of the land, so saving the life of Jeremiah (Jer. 26: 18, and Mic. 3: 12). (b) Quoted when the magi arrived at Jerusalem (Matt. 2: 5, 6; Mic. 5: 2); and (c) by our Lord when sending out his twelve disciples (Matt. 10: 35, 36; Mic. 7: 6).

## Analysis

Some hold the view that the book contains three addresses, each beginning with the word 'Hear'. But, unfortunately for this view, this word is found five times, not three, 1: 2; 3: 1, 9; 6: 1, 2. Like Isaiah, it falls into two clear divisions: Denunciatory (cc. 1-3), then Consolatory (cc. 4-6). It bears a striking resemblance to Isaiah. It has been regarded by some as a summary of the predictions of Isaiah, in fact 'Isaiah in shorthand'; but, of course, it is a book separate and distinct. It falls into four sub-sections.

---

## DENUNCIATORY

**'Who is a God like unto thee'**

**— in Witnessing?**

(cc. 1 to 3; key for this section 1: 2)

1 The prophet and his hearers (1: 1, 2)
2 Practical description of the Lord coming forth in judgment to witness against Israel (1: 3, 5)
3 Cause of the judgment (1: 5)
4 Destruction of Samaria foretold (1: 6, 7)
5 An invasion of Judah (1: 8, 9)
6 And the consequent panic (1: 10-16)
7 Apostasy from God and injustice to man condemned (c. 2)
8 The ruling classes denounced (3: 1-11)
9 Destruction of Jerusalem graphically foretold (3: 12).

## CONSOLATORY

**1 'Who is a God like unto thee'**

**— in Consoling?**

(cc. 4, 5; key 4: 4)

1 Observe the change in tone. The Lord, who witnessed against Israel, is seen here consoling her by declarations of coming glories (4: 1-5)
2 Israel, though scattered, is to be gathered (4: 6-8)
3 And, though the Babylonian captivity was certain, they should be delivered (4: 9-13)
4 All this will come about through Jesus, the everlasting one (5: 1-3)
5 Israel's future glory (5: 5-15).

**2 'Who is a God like unto thee'**

**— in Pleading?**

(c. 6; key 6: 2, 3)

1 This is a most touching chapter. How appealingly the Lord pleads (vv.1-5)
2 He requires a spiritual worship and service (vv.6-8)
3 Sin and evil denounced and judged (vv.9-16)
Note the prophet speaks in v.8 of God's requirements but he has nothing to say about God's gift. We cannot meet God's requirement without first receiving God's great gifts of righteousness and life. Hence Chapter 7.

**3 'Who is a God like unto thee'**

**— in Pardoning?**

(c. 7; key 7: 18)

1 The prophet mourns (vv.1-4)
2 Even the home had been invaded by deceit and hatred (vv.5, 6)
3 The prophet turns to God (v.7), rebukes the enemy (v.8), makes humble confession of Israel's sin (v.9), confidently counts upon God for the future (vv.10-17), and closes by declaring the fulness, freeness and faithfulness of the Lord's pardon.

# 34
# The Book of Nahum

**Key phrase:** 'Utter end'
**Key verses:** 1: 8, 9
**Theme: The awful doom of the apostate**

### Nahum

Nahum, the writer of this book, was a native of Elkosh (1: 1). There is an Elkosh in Assyria, situated a few miles north of the ruins of Nineveh, where a tomb has long been pointed out as that of the prophet; but authorities, for several reasons, reject this place for that of Elkosh in Galilee. This latter place, though in ruins, was pointed out to Jerome as Nahum's by a native guide.

### Historical setting

To get the right historical setting is important to the right understanding of this book. It is clear that Nahum was a native of Galilee, and was contemporary with Hezekiah and Isaiah. Upon the Assyrian invasion and deportation of the ten tribes, he escaped into the territory of Judah, and probably took up his residence in Jerusalem where he witnessed, seven years afterwards, the siege of that city by Sennacherib, and the destruction of the Assyrian host, when 185,000 perished in one night, as recorded in 2 Kings cc. 18, 19. Undoubtedly there are references to this in Nahum 1: 11, etc. Shortly after this event Nahum wrote this book.

### Subject

This book has but one theme, the destruction of Nineveh. It was written about 150 years after the mission of Jonah. The revival, or rather the repentance, at the preaching of Jonah, sincere though it was, was not durable, and had been replaced by a complete and deliberate apostasy from God. They were not merely backsliders: far worse, they were apostates, deliberately rejecting and challenging the God they had accepted and worshipped (see 2 Kgs 18: 25, 30, 35; 19: 10-13). The Lord accepted the haughty Assyrian challenge (19: 22-23), and Nahum was chosen to record the prediction of the final and complete overthrow of Nineveh and her empire — an empire which had been built up by violence and cruel oppression, and which was doomed to perish in a violent and extraordinary way. All this prophecy came to pass eighty-six years afterwards. Nahum's book is one great 'at last'.

### Style

Nahum forms a beautiful, vivid, pictorial poem on the grandeur, power, and justice of God, and on the conflict between Jehovah and this cruel and defiant world empire of Nineveh. A great student of the prophets writes: 'None of the minor prophets seems to equal Nahum in boldness, ardour, and sublimity. His prophecy forms a regular and perfect poem; the exordium is not merely magnificent, it is truly majestic; the preparation for the destruction of Nineveh, and the description of its downfall and desolation, are expressed in the most vivid colours, and are bold and luminous in the highest degree.'

### Message

Its message is two-fold: (1) It is a message of comfort ('Nahum' means 'Comfort') to a harassed and fearful people in peril through the cruel and awful military power of Assyria. Note how comforting 1: 7, 12, 13 would be. (2) It is a message of warning, showing that all that God can do with an apostate people and nation is to destroy it.

### Analysis

The book falls into two sections, introducing us first to the judge, then to the judgment.

---

## THE JUDGE (1: 1-7)

1 The book opens with a declaration of who and what God is, giving 'a sublime and powerful statement of those attributes of God which constitute the basis of all his actions towards the children of men'.
2 Under the figure of a storm is set forth the overwhelming majesty of God.

---

## THE JUDGMENT (1: 8 to 3: 19)

### The Verdict
**(1: 8-14)**
1 Condemned to extinction (vv.8, 9).
2 Nineveh was captured while defenders were drunk (v.10).
3 Without doubt v.11 refers to Rabshakeh (see 2 Kings 18: 17-37).
4 Name to be blotted out (v.14).

### The Application
**(1: 15)**
1 The first chapter closes with a warning to Judah.
2 This appeal to Judah coming after what had been said of Nineveh, is most impressive — God would deal with them severely if they did not turn from the error of their ways.

### The Vision
**(c. 2)**
The picture given of the siege and fall of Nineveh, and the desolation which followed is most vivid and graphic. The prophet sees, and makes his hearers see, all the horrid sights of the tragic scene.

### The Certainty
**(c. 3)**
1 The Victor and the vanquished (vv.1-3).
2 The cause of the overthrow (v.4).
3 The certainty of this judgment (vv.8-10).
4 Various other particulars are here given of the siege.

# 35
# The Book of Habakkuk

Key word: Why?
Key verses: 1: 3, 13
Theme: God's consistency with himself in view of permitted evil

## Literary excellence

1 Viewed simply as literature (though it is infinitely more than that!) this book stands pre-eminent for its literary beauty. It is said that Benjamin Franklin read Habakkuk to a literary circle in Paris, winning their unanimous tribute of admiration for an author of whom not one had ever heard before.

2 Habakkuk's description of the majesty and self-revelation of God in Chapter 3 stands supreme; and the whole of the book is written in a strongly lyrical style approaching nearer to the Psalms in structure than any other of the prophetic writings.

## Who was Habakkuk?

1 What he writes concerning himself, explains the resemblance of his writings to the Psalms. He was not only a prophet (1: 1), but also one of the Levitical choristers in the Temple (3: 19). Beyond this, nothing further is known of the prophet.

2 Judging from 1: 5, 6, which speaks of the Chaldean invasion as still future, though imminent, he must have lived and laboured in the latter part of the reign of Joash (see 2 Kgs 22: 18-20). The invasion took place five years later.

## Grandfather of reformation

1 This prophet is actually the grandfather of the Reformation. The great doctrine of justification by faith Paul learned from Habakkuk, and Luther learned it from Paul.

2 One would conclude that this book must have been a favourite with Paul, for he quotes 1: 5 in his warning to the unbelieving Jews at Antioch (Acts 13: 41), and that famous statement of 2: 4 he quotes three times (Rom. 1: 17; Gal. 3: 11; Heb. 10: 38).

## Conversational

1 This book is unique in that quite two-thirds of it is a conversation between the prophet and his Lord.

2 Habakkuk has been called not only 'the prophet of faith' but also 'the free-thinker among the prophets'. 'He could not square his belief in a good and righteous God with the facts of life as he sees them.' He was troubled with the 'Why?'

3 Yet in all this mystery and perplexity, true to his name (which means 'to embrace', 'to cling'), he clung to God, and, pouring out his difficulties to him in prayer, waited patiently (2: 1) for the divine explanation.

## The First Conversation

1 He was perplexed with the silence and forbearance of God in permitting evil to continue, and pours out his soul to God (1: 1-4)
Prophet's perplexity at —
1 Lord's neglect of his prayers (v.2);
2 And apparent indifference to sin and suffering (vv.3, 4).

2 God answers by stating his silence did not mean ignorance or indifference, but that he was about to bring punishment upon that sinful nation (1: 5-11)
God replied that he —
1 Was about to do something incredible (v.5);
2 That he would use the Chaldeans to chastise Israel for their sin (v.6);
3 And gives a graphic character sketch of the Chaldeans (vv.7-11).

## The Second Conversation

1 The Lord's reply, though it solved one difficulty, raised another, viz: how a pure God could chastise Israel by a nation far worse than themselves (1: 12 to 2: 1).
Prophet declared it difficult to believe that —
1 The eternal and holy God could chasten a sinful people by a people more sinful (vv.12, 13);
2 And permit them to catch men as fishes (vv.14, 15);
3 When they glorified themselves (vv.16, 17).
4 The prophet's patience (2: 1).

2 To this the Lord replies that he was not unmindful of the wickedness of the instrument, and would presently punish them very sorely (2: 2-20)
1 God bade the prophet write very plainly what he was about to say (v.2).
2 What God was about to do would come to pass (v.3).
3 Those counted righteous through their faith would be preserved from those terrible sorrows (v.4).
4 And then God utters five woes against Chaldeans (vv.5-20).

## The Prophet's Hymn and Doxology

Finding all his difficulties solved, and God's 'hush!' taking possession of his soul, he pours out his whole being in a thrilling hymn of prayer, praise, and confidence in God (c. 3).
1 Prophet prays that God would revive his delivering grace (v.2);
2 And that, in the execution of judgment, he would remember mercy (v.2).
3 Then he gives a description of the majesty of the Lord at Sinai, and in going before Israel to possess Canaan (vv.3-15).

4 Remembrance of all this brings rest to his soul (v.16),
5 And confidence in God (vv.17-19).

# 36
# The Book of Zephaniah

Key word: Jealousy
Key verses: 1: 18; 3: 8
Theme: 'I, the Lord, thy God, am a jealous God'

## Writer

Very little is known of Zephaniah, the writer of this book. By 1: 1 we learn that he was probably a prince of the royal house of Judah, being a descendant of Hezekiah. He is supposed to have been a youth. His name means 'Hidden of Jehovah'. Perhaps he had his name in mind when he wrote 2: 3.

## Work

He began his prophetic ministry in the early days of the reign of Josiah (641-610 B.C.). He foretold the doom of Nineveh (2: 13), which came to pass in 625 B.C.; and in 1: 4 he denounces various forms of idolatry, which were swept away by Josiah. Without doubt he was mainly responsible for the revival under Josiah. Tradition states that he had Jeremiah as colleague.

## Key words

There are three. (1) 'The day of the Lord' is mentioned seven times and forms one key to the study of this book. (2) 'In the midst' is another striking key phrase. (3) But *the* key word is 'Jealousy'. There is a jealousy which must never be associated with God, a jealousy which is always suspicious of faithlessness, and constantly on the lookout for evidences of it. Milton speaks of such jealousy as 'a lover's hell'. What a hell on earth is that home wherein such jealousy exists! But there is another kind of jealousy which is the natural outcome of love, and that is the nature of God's jealousy. He so loves his people that he cannot bear a rival, and must have their whole-hearted devotion; and he will do everything he can to secure this, even going to the length of awful judgments, as here.

## Contents

On taking up the book one is simply appalled at its contents — stern denunciation, dire threatenings, nothing but mutterings and threatenings of wrath — but remembering Cowper's fine phrase that chastisement is 'the graver countenance of love', we see in all this the proof of God's love. But if the book begins with woe, it ends with singing; though the first two sections are full of gloom and sadness, the last section contains the sweetest love song in the Old Testament.

---

## The Lord 'in the midst' for JUDGMENT (1: 1 to 3: 8, key 3: 5 with 1: 7)

**1 The devouring fire of the Lord's jealousy kindled in 'the whole land' of Israel**
**(1: 1 to 2: 3; 3: 1-7; note 1: 18)**

1 Threat of judgment (1: 2-7)
2 Those on whom the judgment will fall (1: 8-13)
3 Nearness of the day of the Lord (1: 14-18) (Partially fulfilled in the invasion of Nebuchadnezzar, but its full and complete fulfilment is yet future.)
4 Call to repentance (2: 1-3)
5 The sad moral state of Jerusalem in the prophet's time (3: 1-7)

**2 The devouring fire of the Lord's jealousy kindled over 'all the earth' amongst Gentiles**
**(2: 4-15; with note 3: 8)**

1 Judgment on Israel's local enemies, literally fulfilled in those days (2: 4-15)
2 Judgment on Israel's world-wide enemies yet to be fulfilled (3: 8, with 2: 10, 11)
**(Truly wonderful and amazing verses.)**

## The Lord 'in the midst' for SALVATION (3: 9-20; key 3: 15, 17)

**The devouring fire of the Lord's jealousy *quenched*, and the Lord at 'rest in his love' (3: 9-20; note 3: 17)**

1 Israel's repentance (v.9) followed by Israel's restoration (v.10) humility (vv.11, 12) sanctification (v.13) rejoicing (v.14) and deliverance (v.15).
2 Note the singing of the Lord (3: 17).
3 The Lord told Job (38: 7) that when he laid the foundations of the earth 'the morning stars sang together and all the sons of God shouted for joy', but God was silent.
4 The first time we read of his singing, is in connection with redemption (Psalm 105: 43, margin).

5 Was Matthew 26: 30 the last time he sang? The last time he sang was no later than the last conversion!
6 And when Israel is restored he will sing again.

# 37
# The Book of Haggai

Key phrase: 'The word of the Lord'
Key verse: 1: 13
Theme: God first in life and service

**Time**
'The second year of Darius' in which Haggai prophesied was 520 B.C. (Confucius, the celebrated Chinese philosopher, flourished in China at this time).

**Writer**
We know nothing about Haggai beyond the fact that he was a prophet working in conjunction with Zechariah. He was probably born at Babylon during the captivity. His name means 'My feast', and may have been given to him in joyous anticipation of the return from captivity. He began to prophesy two months before Zechariah; but while Zechariah prophesied for three years, Haggai only prophesied three months and twenty-four days.

**Occasion**
Sixteen years had passed since the return from captivity. Ezra c. 3 states that the first thought and care of the people was the rebuilding of the altar and the Temple; but difficulties cropped up. Eventually, political intrigues stopped the work, and the zeal and enthusiasm of the people died away in the face of these prolonged difficulties; and although the storm spent itself and passed by, the workers did not return to their work. Then came a season of distress — the harvest failed, there was drought, and trouble and sorrow (1: 6, 9-11). Haggai was sent to interpret the calamity, and urge them to have done with their sinful sloth and despondency. The result was good. In twenty-four days the people began to re-build. Then other comforting and cheering messages were given.

**Style**
Each book in the Bible has a style of its own. The style of Haggai is plain, simple, curt, business-like. He was fond of interrogation (e.g. 1: 4; 2: 3, 12, 13), which compels thought and attention. Certain phrases he often repeats, as 'saith the Lord', and 'Lord of hosts', twelve times each; 'Consider' quite four times. 'The word of the Lord' occurs five times, and marks the division of the book. There were five messages, delivered on separate and distinct occasions.

**Message**
1 'God first' in life and service, is the message of the Book. It is an Old Testament commentary, and illustration, of 1 Corinthians 15: 58.
2 Haggai stands before us a model worker for God, a pattern for us to copy:
(a) He effaced himself. He spends no time in giving details about his life and service. He exalts his Lord.
(b) He ever had a 'thus saith the Lord'. He was the Lord's messenger.
(c) He not only rebuked, but cheered; not only criticised, but commended and stimulated by word and example.
(d) He not only preached, but practised. He lent a hand, see Ezra 5: 1, 2.

---

**1 September 1st**
**A stern message of**
## Rebuke
**(1: 1-11)**
1 Disheartened, and disinclined for work, they tried to excuse themselves by a mistake in the reckoning of years (v.2).
2 Calamity stated and interpreted (vv.6, 11).
3 People urged to work (v.8).

**2 September 24th**
**A comforting message of**
## Commendation
**(1: 12-15)**
1 Rebuke has desired effect (v.12).
2 At once, Haggai had given to him from the Lord, one very short but most comforting message (v.13).
3 And that message had a stirring effect (v.14).

**3 October 21st**
**A cheering message of**
## Encouragement
**(2: 1-9)**
1 As they laboured, they were disheartened by the fact that, owing to their poverty, the Temple would be inferior to Solomon's.
2 Haggai cheered them by declaring that its glory would be greater than the former one. Jesus stood in it.

**4 December 24th**
**An assuring message concerning Cleansing and**
## Blessing
**(2: 10-19)**
1 By question and answer, Haggai dwelt on the impurity of the people.
2 But that impurity had been removed.
3 Now there was blessing for them.

**5 December 24th**
**A steadying message concerning**
## Safety
**(2: 20-23)**
1 Evidently 2:6, 7 had troubled them.
2 By the figure of the 'signet', they were taught how the Lord esteemed, valued, and cared for them;
3 And also, how safe they were in troublous times.

# 38
# The Book of Zechariah

**Key phrase: 'I am jealous'**
**Key verses: 1: 14; 2: 8; 8: 2 RV**
**Theme: God's love and care for his people**

## Author

1 Zechariah, the prophet of restoration and glory, was probably born in Babylon. The difference between Ezra 5: 1; 6: 14 and Zechariah 1: 1 can be easily explained. Probably his father died in his infancy, and then his grandfather Iddo (Neh. 12: 4, 16) reared him.

2 He was thus priest as well as prophet. The three names are very significant when put together — Zechariah, 'Jehovah remembers'; Berechiah, 'Jehovah blesses'; Iddo, 'the appointed time'. Thus these three names form a key to the meaning of the book. Note the key words of the book, 'Jealous', 'Jealousy'.

## Mission

1 He was contemporary with Haggai, being the younger of the two (2: 4) and his mission was to encourage the despondent.

2 He encouraged the disheartened by prophesying, in glowing terms, of the glory to come to Israel in far off ages.

3 This is the divine method of encouragement — taking our eyes off the sad present to the glories of the future. He exercised his ministry for three years.

## Style

Zechariah was one of the greatest of ancient inspired seers, and his fourteen chapters are full of the most striking visions recorded in the Old Testament. He was a great poet, and thus a fitting companion to plain, practical Haggai.

## Analysis

1 It is in two principal divisions — the first division falls into three sections, the second into two. The book consists of five separate and distinct messages.

2 'Instead of this book being all fulfilled prophecy, as some would say, it is indeed mostly unfulfilled, and even some of the prophecies which, on the surface seem to have seen a fulfilment, were only in part realised.'

---

## First Division — APOCALYPTIC (cc. 1 to 8)

### First Message
**(1: 1-6)**

An earnest call to repentance. He reminded them of their fathers' sin (v.2), and of the captivity which resulted (v.6), and exhorted them to flee from those sins (v.4). In lamenting their departed greatness, they must not forget the cause. (Note: 'take hold' in v.6, is in margin of AV/KJV and in RV 'Overtake'. Judgments as well as blessings follow and overtake us.)

### Second Message
**(1:7 to 6:15)**

Eight visions, all given in one night, and all designed for encouragement.
**1 The Material Side of Future Prosperity**
Myrtle Trees (1: 7-17) Israel, lowly and downtrodden, watched and prayed for.
Horns and Smiths (1: 18-21) Foretelling the overthrow of Israel's enemies.
Measuring Line (c. 2) Revealing the glorious prosperity of Jerusalem, as result of the overthrow of the enemies.
**2 The Spiritual Side of Future Prosperity**
Joshua, the Priest (c. 3) Picture of national pollution, cleansing, and restoration of nation to priestly service.
Candlestick (c. 4) Result is that Israel is able to be God's lightbearer to the world.

Flying Roll (5: 1-4) Israel becomes a moral force in the world through the Word of God.
Ephah (5: 5-11) Application of the law of God.
Four Chariots (6: 1-8) Agency at work for Israel. Conclusion, symbolic crowning.

### Third Message
**(cc. 7, 8)**

1 This third message was uttered nearly two years later.
2 It is a fourfold answer to an enquiry made by a deputation from Babylon concerning the necessity of observing certain feasts they (not God) had instituted.
3 The fast of the fifth month observed the destruction of the Temple, and that of the seventh month was kept on the anniversary of the murder of Gedaliah (Jer. c. 41).
4 Answer first (7: 1-7); second (7: 8-14); third (8: 1-17); fourth (8: 18-23).

---

## Second Division — PROPHETIC (cc. 9 to 14)

### Fourth and Fifth Messages
**(cc. 9 to 11, and 12 to 14)**

1 The prophecies of this fourth message have had a partial, but yet not a full and complete fulfilment (see 9: 8).
2 The prophecies of the fifth message are all wholly future.
3 The prophecies are not in chronological order.
4 Note concerning the king:
(a) The coming of the king (9: 9), only partially fulfilled.
(b) The rejection of the king
    Price paid (11: 12, 13).
    Shepherd slain (13: 6, 7).
    Scattering of people (11: 7-11).
(c) The second advent of the king (14: 3-8).
(d) The victories of the king (9: 8; 12: 1-9, 10-14; 13: 1-5).
(e) The programme of the king (9: 10-17; c. 10; 14: 9-21).

# 39
# The Book of Malachi

Key phrase: 'Ye say'
Key verse: 3: 1
Theme: Remember, repent, return, rehearse

**Angel's name**
1 Malachi is the unknown prophet with the angelic name. Nothing is known of him. Some even think that his name is unknown, Malachi being only a title descriptive of his official position, meaning 'My angel' or 'Messenger'.
2 He not only bore this name, but unlike many of us, he was proud of his name, loving to repeat it. Speaking of Levi, as an example of the true priesthood, he says 'he is the messenger of the Lord of hosts' (2: 7); he described John the Baptist as 'God's messenger', and speaks of our Lord as 'the messenger of the covenant' (3: 1).

**Dialogue**
1 This book is notable for its dialogue style. One evidence of a backslidden state is the hyper-critical spirit. God's people were in a sad spiritual condition, and consequently were prepared to call into question anything and everything, even God's own statements. All their words of criticism had been noted by the Lord — 'Ye say' is met with quite a dozen times (1: 2, 6, 7, 12, 13; 2: 14, 17; 3: 7, 8, 13, 14). He keeps account also of the statements of others (1: 4).
2 But God not only took note of their sayings — he combated them, as even a casual study of the above texts will show.

**A Portrait**
1 Malachi was the last of the prophets. 'His prophecies therefore have a grave and solemn importance, and on two accounts. First as showing the state of the remnant who, in the tender mercy of God, had been brought back from Babylon; and secondly, because of the correspondence of the position of this remnant with that of God's people at the present moment. As there was nothing between them (and the coming of Christ,) so there is nothing to intervene between ourselves and the expectation of the Lord's return.'
2 In Israel's state, as revealed by Malachi, we have a telling portrait of our own time and age.

**Message**
Remember his love; repent of your sins; return to him; rehearse to one another his love, grace, and promised advent.

**Analysis**
The book falls into two sections and three subsections, as follows:

---

## EXPOSTULATION (cc. 1, 2)

### A Message of Love
(1: 1-5)
1 God's declaration of his love for Israel (v.2),
2 Israel blindly questions that love for them (v.2),
3 The Lord condescends to give one of the many proofs (vv.3-5).
(Note. In the Old Testament we get the declaration of God's love for Israel (v.2); in the New Testament we have announced God's love for the world [John 3: 16].)

### A Message of Rebuke
(1: 6 to 2: 17)
**To the Priests**
1 Did not give God reverence and honour due to him (v.6),
2 Offered to God what they would not dare offer the governor (v.8),
3 Refused to work except for gain (v.10),
4 God's determination that, in spite of Israel's failure, his name should be great (v.11),
5 Their utter failure (2: 1-9).

**To the People**
1 Guilty of sins against one another (2: 10).
2 Against God in the family (2: 11-17).

---

## PREDICTION (cc. 3, 4)

### A Message of Hope
(cc. 3, 4)
A Series of prophecies concerning:
1 John the Baptist's advent and work (3: 1)
2 The coming and work of the Lord, all yet in the future (3: 1-6)
3 The sad state of his people prior to his coming (3: 7-15)
4 Yet even then there will be a faithful remnant (3: 16-18)
5 The day of the Lord (4: 1)
6 His advent has no terrors for his faithful ones (4: 2-4)
7 Elijah to come again before the day of the Lord (4: 5).

# ANALYSES of the BOOKS of the NEW TESTAMENT

| Book | Key Word or Phrase | Theme |
|---|---|---|
| MATTHEW | KINGDOM | Jesus as the Messiah King |
| MARK | STRAIGHTWAY | Jesus as the servant |
| LUKE | SON OF MAN | Jesus as the ideal man |
| JOHN | BELIEVE | Jesus as the eternal Son of God |
| ACTS | BEGAN | The work continued by the Spirit |
| ROMANS | RIGHTEOUSNESS | Justification by faith |
| 1 CORINTHIANS | 'OUR LORD' | The Lordship of Christ |
| 2 CORINTHIANS | COMFORT, MINISTRY | The nature of Comfort: the performance of Ministry |
| GALATIANS | FAITH | Christ the deliverer from the law |
| EPHESIANS | THE CHURCH | The church, the body of Christ |
| PHILIPPIANS | ALL | Christian unity to be maintained at all cost |
| COLOSSIANS | HE IS THE HEAD | The supreme glory and dignity of Christ |
| 1 THESSALONIANS | WAIT FOR HIS SON | The Coming of the Lord *for* his people |
| 2 THESSALONIANS | DAY OF THE LORD | The Coming of the Lord *with* his people |
| 1 TIMOTHY | 'HOW THOU OUGHTEST TO BEHAVE' | Designed to accomplish (1 Tim. 4: 12) |
| 2 TIMOTHY | ASHAMED | Loyalty to the Lord and to truth |
| TITUS | THYSELF A PATTERN | God's ideal for the Christian church |
| PHILEMON | RECEIVE | The practice of Christian forgiveness |
| HEBREWS | BETTER | A right conception of the glory of Christ |
| JAMES | FAITH, WORKS | Faith shown by its works |
| 1 PETER | SUFFERING | How we may suffer to the glory of God |
| 2 PETER | REMEMBRANCE | Purity and loyalty amidst corruption and apostasy |
| 1 JOHN | KNOW, FELLOWSHIP | The life of fellowship with God |
| 2 JOHN | TRUTH | Truth must be received and obeyed |
| 3 JOHN | FELLOW-HELPERS | Hospitality: domineering leadership |
| JUDE | KEEP, KEPT | Keeping the faith and being kept |
| REVELATION | 'THE REVELATION OF JESUS CHRIST' | Jesus, the gloriously triumphant one |

# 40
# The Gospel according to Matthew

**Key word: Kingdom**
**Key verses: 1: 1; 27: 37**
**Theme: Jesus as the Messiah King**

## Value
Renan, the sceptic, described this Gospel, as 'the most important book of Christendom — the most important book that has ever been written'. Quite agreed as to its importance, we would prefer to say 'one of the most important'.

## Writer
1 It was written by Matthew the converted publican (9: 9). He is called Levi in Mark 2: 14. Evidently he was re-named Matthew by our Lord.
2 It is only in his Gospel that the despised name of publican is associated with his apostolic name of Matthew. (Matthew means 'gift of God'.)
3 He seems to have been a man of means. Modestly he makes no reference to the 'great feast' he made on his call to the ministry (Luke 5: 29), or his great sacrifice in following Christ. But for this authorship, Matthew would have been one of the least known of the apostles.

## Purpose
1 The book was written originally in Hebrew, and was specially designed for the use of the Jews, consequently the Old Testament is often quoted.

2 One characteristic word in this book is 'fulfilled'. He makes no less than sixty references to the Old Testament writings as fulfilled in Christ.

3 There is no discord between the four Gospels as some imagine. Each wrote with a specific purpose in view. Each gives a different portrait of the Lord Jesus. The portrait Matthew gives of Jesus is that of king. The word 'kingdom' is met with fifty-five times, 'kingdom of heaven' thirty-two times, 'son of David' seven times.

4 This book shows that the mission of Jesus was primarily to the Jews (10: 5, 6; 15: 24). The 'gospel of the kingdom' preached by Jesus and his disciples (4: 23; 10: 7) was not identical with the gospel preached today; the former is the good news that God was about to set up on the earth a political and spiritual kingdom, ruled over by Jesus, as the son of David, whereas the latter has to do with God's spiritual sway. The gospel of the kingdom was preached up to the rejection and crucifixion of Jesus, but will again be preached just before the great tribulation (24: 14) and second advent of Jesus as king. The gospel we preach today is good news concerning salvation through Christ, and the calling out of a people for him, viz. the gospel of the grace of God.

## THE KING

### His birth
(cc. 1, 2)
The genealogy and birth of the king with the worship of the eastern kings (wise men); the persecution by Herod the usurper.
The Lord Jesus is last in Jewish history whose descent from the royal line of David can be clearly established.

### His testing
(4: 1-11)
1 Here the Lord Jesus vanquished the tempter, refusing to gain the kingdom in any way but God's.
2 'The first Adam fell in Eden surrounded by creature comforts; the second Adam conquered in the wilderness, his body enfeebled by long abstinence.'

### His proclamation
(4: 12-25)
1 Jesus did not come to found the church but the kingdom. Here, his royal proclamation.
2 The kingdom of God is made up of all in heaven and earth who submit; the entrance into that kingdom is by new birth (John c. 3). The kingdom of heaven is visible establishment of the kingdom of God on earth.

### His laws
(cc. 5 to 7)
1 The sermon on the mount is only for disciples, the code of laws especially for Christ's earthly kingdom, which he will set up by and by, though it has a message for us.
2 The sermon on the mount has a moral application to Christians.

### His rejection
(11: 20 to 20: 34)
1 A section of great importance. Israel having practically rejected its king, the establishment of the kingdom is postponed; Jesus, for the first time, gives hint of a new departure, the creation of a new society — the church.
2 Note 12: 14, followed by the 'mystery' teaching of c. 13.

### His death and resurrection
(cc. 26 to 28)
1 Jesus was slain because he declared he was king. (Note specially 27: 11, 12, 29, 37, and 42.)
2 The rending of the veil (27: 51) followed the rending of the heart of Christ.

### His forerunner
(c. 3)
1 All notable persons in the East have forerunners, so Jesus.
2 John Baptist announced imminence of the kingdom, and baptized the king.

### His ministry
(8: 1 to 11: 19)
1 The king actively at work healing and teaching among his people Israel.
2 Note RV of 8: 6: 'servant' is rendered 'boy' — a most affectionate term, showing the servant had endeared himself to his master.

### His entry
(cc. 21 to 25)
1 The official entry of the king into his capital, and his final, public rejection.
2 Note 25: 41. No earthly judge makes the criminal's doom a matter of personal relationship to himself — Christ does. To depart from Christ means to depart from hope.

# 41
# The Gospel according to Mark

Key word: Straightway
Key verse: 10: 45
Theme: Jesus as the servant

## Writer
1 The writer of this second Gospel was not an apostle, but only an associate of the apostles, just an ordinary worker.
2 He was the son of one of the Marys of the New Testament, who evidently was a person in comfortable circumstances (Acts 12: 12).
3 He was nephew of Barnabas, and it was owing to him that Paul and Barnabas disagreed (Acts 15: 36-41).
4 It is thought that Mark was converted through Peter; at any rate he became the companion of Peter, and recorded his utterances.

## Origin
The early Fathers, notably Clement of Alexandria, describe the impression made by the graphic preaching of Peter, the anxiety of his hearers to possess in writing what had delighted them when heard, their coming to Mark, Peter's companion, with the entreaty that he would record for them his master's words, Mark's compliance with the request, and Peter's apostolic sanction to the work. Justin Martyr refers to it as the *Memoirs*, or *Gospel of St Peter*.

## Purpose
1 It was written, so it is believed, at Rome for the Romans. Consequently (1) there are very few references to the Old Testament scriptures. (2) Jewish words are explained (3: 17; 5: 41; 7: 11, 34; 14: 36); also Jewish customs (7: 3, 4; 14: 12; 15: 42). (3) Latin words are frequently used, e.g. Legion, Centurion, etc.
2 The whole tone of the book reflects Peter's energetic and impulsive nature, and thus was admirably fitted for the Roman citizen, who was a 'hustler' — a man of action.
3 The portrait it gives of the Lord Jesus is that of the Servant, the ideal worker. As the average Roman cared little for doctrine or teaching, but a great deal for action, in this Gospel the deeds of our Lord are emphasised and not his words.

## Analysis
This book almost baffles any attempt at analysis, it is so crowded with incidents. Yet we see five clear divisions.

## THE SERVANT

### His arrival and identity (1: 1-11)
1 There is no genealogy, birth, infancy — out of place in description of a servant.
2 He is a servant to all, not merely to the Jew.
3 The servant is the Son of God, declared (v.1), announced (v.2).
4 He is fitted for his ministry by the Spirit.

**Lesson:**
Nor can we serve God acceptably unless we are his children through faith in Christ Jesus, and have the witness and enduement of the Spirit.

### His fidelity (1: 12, 13)
1 Only here is it recorded that in temptation, he 'was with the wild beasts'.
2 David, before he entered upon his service, did battle with wild beasts (1 Sam. 17: 34-36).
3 The divine servant was loyal to God.

**Lesson:**
We must be loyal to God, and, by his grace, live the overcoming life, before we can be of real service.

### The character and nature of his work (1: 14 to 13: 37)
1 The Wise Servant — seen in his setting others to work (1: 14-20; 2: 13, 14; 3: 14-19; 6: 7-13).
2 The Servant with authority over demons, elements, death, and in teaching (1: 21-28; 4: 35-41; c. 5; 6: 47-51; 9: 14-29).
3 A tender, loving ministry of compassion (1: 29-34, 40-45; 5:41; 6: 34; 8: 2; 10: 13-16, 21).
4 His service the outcome of prayer (1: 35; 6: 46; 14: 32-41).
5 His a bustling, active service without fuss or fret (1: 36-39).
6 A servant, never off duty, even in his own house (2: 1-12, 15-22).

7 A costly service, meaning much grief (3: 5), many sighs (7: 34; 8: 12), and death (8: 27-38).
8 A self-denying service (3: 20; 6: 31).
9 As servant, teaching divine truth in simple language (c. 4; 9: 33-37; 12: 1-12; 1: 22, see 12: 37).
10 He continued in service, despised, misunderstood (6: 1-6).
11 Service which took notice of the service of others (9: 38, 40; 12: 41-44).

**Lesson:**
He is the Pattern: may our service be more like his.

### His obedience to death (cc. 14, 15)
1 Like the ox, he was ready for service or sacrifice: he did both.
2 His dying was invaluable service, and for us!
3 Note 14: 51, 52 and the interesting supposition that this was Mark himself.

### Risen and glorified (c. 16)
1 He arose! and his resurrection can be viewed in the light of service.
2 Note the significance of 'and Peter' (v.7).
3 Observe in v.20 he is still the worker, in co-operation with his servants.

# 42
# The Gospel according to Luke

Key word: Son of Man
Key verse: 23: 47
Theme: Jesus as the ideal man

## Writer

Luke, the writer of this Gospel, according to Eusebius, was a native of Antioch, in Syria. He was a Gentile. His name, an abbreviated form of Lucanus, is thought by some to prove he was a Greek. He was an educated man, and followed the profession of a physician. The first mention of him as fellow worker of Paul is in Acts 16: 10.

## Purpose

It was written for Greek readers — in the first instance, sent to a personal friend — after exhaustive research, and was intended to stop the spread of spurious Gospels and false accounts of the life of lives. As Luke was companion to Paul, it is believed that he incorporated in this book the substance of that great apostle's preaching.

## Message

1 Renan, the sceptic, declared that this was 'the most beautiful book in the world'. It is one that artists revel in: more pictures have been painted from it than from any of the others.

2 That this book was intended for Greek readers is the clue to its message. The Grecian ideal of perfect manliness differed from that of the Roman. While the Romans felt it to be their mission to govern, the Greeks felt it theirs to educate, elevate, and perfect man. The ideal of the Roman was military glory and governmental authority, but the Greek's was wisdom and beauty.

3 The portrait Luke draws of Jesus is that of the perfect man, the one who more than meets the highest ideals of the Greeks. While he speaks of the deity of Christ, the emphasis is placed upon the perfect manhood of Christ. His character as revealed in this Gospel is intensely human, as we shall see in the following study. He is 'Son of man' as well as the 'Son of God'.

## THE MAN

### 'Made like unto his brethren' (cc. 1 to 3, compare Heb. 2: 17)

1 One with us in descent from Adam, fountain head of humanity (3: 23, 38).
2 One with us in common human relationships, with all attendant duties (first two chapters deal with the cousins of Mary).
3 One with us in our shame by baptism (in submitting to baptism he lost his character in the estimation of the Jewish world).
Note: here preserved the first precious germs of Christian hymnology (1: 68-79; 1: 46, 55; 2: 14; 2: 29, 32).

### 'Tempted like as we are' (4: 1-13; compare Heb. 4: 15)

Luke views the temptation from the standpoint of man: 'The devil challenged the first Adam, the second Adam challenges the devil. The devil ruined the first man; the devil was spoiled by the man Christ Jesus. The first Adam involved the race in his defeat; the last Adam included the race in his victory.'

### 'Touched with the feeling of our infirmities' (4: 14 to 19: 28; compare Heb. 4: 15)

THE LORD JESUS AS:
**The man of cosmopolitan interests.** This Gospel gives those incidents which show his interest in the whole human race (2: 10; 2: 31, 32; 17: 18; 19: 2).
**The man of wisdom,** as shown in teaching (4: 14, 15, 32; 5: 30, 39; c. 6; 10: 25-37; 20: 2-8).
**The man of ability** (4: 33-37; cc. 5, 8; 9: 37-43).
**The man full of human sympathy** for the fallen and despised (5: 27-39; 7: 36, 37); for the bereaved (7: 11; 8: 42; 9: 38 (Note 'only'); for the despondent (7: 19); for the diseased (4: 38-41; 5: 12; c. 7).

**The man of prayer:** showing absolute dependence upon God in all great crises (3: 21; 5: 16; 6: 12; 9: 18, 29; 11: 1, 2; 9: 29).
**The sociable man** (7: 36; 11: 37; 14: 1; 19: 7).
**The man of beauty and glory** (9: 28-36).
(Note, too, the strong human element in all Luke's parables.)

### As our kinsman, redeeming us (19: 28 to 23: 56)

1 As the patriot, weeping over Jerusalem (19: 41).
2 As man, receiving angel's ministry, in answer to prayer (22: 43).
3 As our kinsman, performing the kinsman's part (See Lev. 25: 47-55; Ruth c. 2; 3: 10-18; 4: 1-10).

### Still man in resurrection and ascension glory (c. 24)

1 The risen Lord still man.
2 As man walking to Emmaus with two men.
3 As man, eating in the upper room, showing his still perfect humanity.
4 Ascending in the act of blessing.
(Note the book begins and ends with rejoicing, all in connection with Jesus.)

# 43
# The Gospel according to John

Key word: Believe
Key verse: 20: 31
Theme: Jesus as the eternal Son of God

## Writer

1 John, the writer of this Gospel, was the son of a master-fisherman (his father had 'hired servants' Mark 1: 20) and of Salome, one of the women who ministered to the Lord of their substance (Matt. 27: 55, 56; Luke 8: 3); from this, and the fact that he had a home of his own in Jerusalem (John 19:

27), it is quite evident he was in comfortable circumstances.
2 Though of a contemplative character he was of hasty and uncertain temper (called a 'son of thunder') until grace took him in hand, and then the lion became a lamb. He became the apostle of love. Evidently he was the youngest of our Lord's apostles, and outlived all the others.

## The book

1 It is the last one of all the inspired writings, written quite fifty years after our Lord's ascension, and is the deepest and most profound of all.
2 On the European continent it is called the 'bosom of Christ', because it reveals the very heart of Christ, the very bosom of the eternal.

## Purpose

1 According to the early Fathers it was written and published at Ephesus, at the request of the apostle Andrew and the Asiatic bishops, to combat certain errors then prevalent concerning the deity of Christ. This is important to notice.

2 Its keyword is 'Believe'. In this Gospel, Jesus Christ is presented as the one whom we are to believe; in John's Epistles the one whom we are to love; and in the Revelation the one for whom we are to wait. But believe what? The deity of the man Christ Jesus. Note 20: 31.

## Peculiarities

Two peculiarities of this Gospel may be noted. (1) The occurrence of the word 'Jew'. It is found only once in Matthew, twice in Mark, twice in Luke, but over sixty times in John. (2) There are only eight miracles (more properly 'signs') recorded, all showing the power of Christ's Word, and of his Word alone.

## Portrait

The portrait drawn for us of Jesus is that of 'the only begotten of the Father'. John shows what it was that convinced men and women of all classes and positions that Jesus was God. The materials he uses in his Gospel are altogether fresh, kept in reserve by God.

---

## THE SON OF GOD

### Before his incarnation (1: 1-14)

1 God did not send him into the world that he might become his son; he is the eternal Son.
2 This Gospel begins like the book of Genesis.
3 Gentiles would understand 'the Word', for they used a similar phrase when speaking of their deities.
4 'In the beginning was the Word' prior to all created things; Jesus is no part of creation.
5 'Word was with God' — another person; Jesus was not God alone.

### Revealed by his deeds and words (1: 15 to 12: 50)

John points out what convinced the people of Christ's deity —
1 The Baptist discovered it through baptism with the Spirit (1: 33).
2 Nathaniel was convinced by Christ's omniscience (1: 48, 49).
3 His disciples convinced by his first miracle — water into wine (2: 11).
4 By cleansing of the Temple, and many unrecorded miracles, numbers of Jews acknowledged him divine (2: 23).
5 Jesus reveals himself to Nicodemus (3: 13-16).
6 The Baptist's four remarkable testimonies (3: 25-36).
7 Jesus reveals himself to the Samaritan woman (4: 26).

8 Samaritans accept him so (4: 41, 42).
9 Nobleman convinced when he found his word as effectual as his presence (4: 53).
10 Opposition because he called God his father (5: 17, 18).
11 Many convinced by miracle of loaves (6: 14).
12 By 6: 35; 8: 12, 58; 10: 9, 11; 11: 25; 14: 6; 15: 1 Jesus declares himself the completed revelation of the great 'I am' of the Old Testament.
13 Jesus reveals himself to the healed man (9: 35-38).
14 Martha's confession (11: 27) and effect of raising of Lazarus (11: 45).
15 Jesus at last acknowledged divine by Jew (12: 12-19) and Gentile (12: 20).

### Revealing himself more fully to his own (cc. 13 to 17)

1 Finally rejected by representatives of the Jewish nation (11: 47-53). Jesus no longer openly declares himself to the world (11: 54).
2 Now he manifests himself fully to his disciples, so that their conviction as to his deity is deepened.

### Slain (cc. 18, 19)

1 Note the effect of one flash of his divinity in 18: 6.
2 By 19: 7 we see he was slain not only because he declared himself king, but because he claimed equality with God.

### His claim fully established by his resurrection (cc. 20, 21)

1 Read Romans 1: 4 No greater proof of divinity could have been given than by resurrection.
2 Note (20: 17) the first time the Lord called his disciples by the tender name 'Brethren'.

# 44
# The Acts of the Apostles

**Key word: Began**
**Key verses: 1: 1 (message); 1: 8 (analysis)**
**Theme: How the work Jesus 'began' was, and is, continued by him through the Spirit.**

## Deeds of Christ

1 According to Daniel Crawford, the picturesque Bantu title for the Acts of the Apostles is: *Words concerning Deeds.*

2 But whose deeds? Its present title is hardly correct, as it deals with only two of the apostles, Peter and Paul. It was known in ancient times as the 'Gospel of the Holy Spirit', and 'Gospel of Resurrection'. It has been called 'The Acts of the Holy Spirit', and that is true; but its correct title is 'The Acts of the Ascended and Glorified Lord'. 1: 1 gives the clue to its message. The Gospels record the life of Jesus in the flesh; Acts records his life in the Spirit. In this book we see the risen and ascended Lord still living and working on by the Holy Spirit through his disciples. Luke, in his Gospel, told us what 'Jesus *began* both to do and teach'; in this book we have a summary of what he continued to do, and is still doing.

## Message

Acts gives prominence to the Lord Jesus. *He* is *the* worker. Trace this fact in the Book: the Lord Jesus as — (1) Commander and Instructor of his people (1: 2-9); (2) The great hope of the church (1: 10, 11); (3) Guide of his people in church matters in times of perplexity (1: 24; 10: 13-16; 16: 10; 22: 18-21); (4) Bestower of the Holy Ghost (2: 33); (5) Burden of all sermons and addresses (2: 22-36; 3: 13-15; 4: 10-33; 5: 30; 6: 14; 8: 5,35; 10: 36 etc); (6) The one who added to the church (2: 47); (7) The only hope for a perishing world (4: 12); (8) The active partner in our service (3: 16, 26: 18: 9, 10); (9) Personal agent in the conversion of Saul (9: 3-6); (10) Encourager of his much tried ones (7: 55, 56; 23: 11).

## Orderliness

1 This is the only unfinished book in the Bible. Note how abruptly it closes: but how else could it close? How can there be a complete account of a person's life and work so long as he lives! And the Lord Jesus still lives!
2 Yet in this incomplete book there is system and order. 1: 8 is the key to the analysis. The entire book records the fulfilment of that prophecy, showing how the work began in Jerusalem, then spread 'to all Judea and Samaria', and eventually reached 'the uttermost parts of the earth'.
3 The book opens with the preaching of the Gospel in Jerusalem, the great ecclesiastical centre of the Jewish nation, and closes with the preaching in Rome, the great centre of the world's power.
4 Note that at the inauguration of each of these widening circles of influence there is a marked outpouring of the Holy Spirit, and an act of divine judgment.

---

**From Pentecost to death of Stephen**
### The Lord at work in 'Jerusalem'

**(cc. 1 to 7)**
1 Work at Jerusalem inaugurated by an outpouring of the Holy Spirit and judgment (2: 1; 5: 1-11).
2 Note. Ascension of our Lord (2: 1-11) (Out of sight, but not out of mind or touch!); ten days waiting for the Spirit (1: 12-14); appointment of an apostle (1: 15-26); pentecost and founding of church (c. 2); lame man healed, and sequel (c. 3); first persecution (c. 4); judgment (c. 5), Deacons (c. 6), Stephen (c. 7).

**Persecution by Paul, to his conversion**
### The Lord at work in 'Judea and Samaria'

**(cc. 8, 9)**
1 Work in this wider sphere inaugurated by an outpouring of the Spirit (8: 17), and threatened judgment (8: 22-24).
2 Note. Persecution under Saul (8: 1-4); Ministry of Philip (8: 5-40).
3 Conversion of Saul (9: 1-30).
4 Further ministry of Peter (9: 32-43).

**Paul's ministry, to imprisonment**
### The Lord at work to 'uttermost parts'

**(cc. 10 to 28)**
1 Work in this important section inaugurated by an outpouring of the Spirit and judgment (10: 44-48; 13: 6-13).
2 Conversion of Cornelius, and sequel (10: 1 to 11:18).
3 The church at Antioch (11: 19-30).
4 Peter's arrest and deliverance (c. 12).
5 Paul's first missionary journey (13: 1 to 15: 35).
6 Paul's second missionary journey (15: 36 to 18: 22).
7 Paul's third missionary journey (18: 22 to 21: 17).
8 Paul's imprisonment (21: 18 to 28: 31).

# 45
# The Epistle to the Romans

Key word: Righteousness
Key verses: 1: 16, 17
Theme: Justification by faith, its method and result.

## The epistle

This epistle was written to the Christians of Rome in the month of February, A.D. 58, at Corinth, in the house of a wealthy Corinthian Christian, called Gaius (16: 23), by Paul, who had as amanuensis, Tertius (16: 22), and was taken to Rome by a well-to-do widow, named Phoebe, who went there on some private business (16: 1, 2).

## Opinions

This epistle has ever been considered as Paul's masterpiece, whether judged from an intellectual or theological standpoint, and the greatest of men have ever valued it most highly. It is said that Chrysostom had this epistle read to him once a week; that Coleridge considered it to be 'the most profound work ever written'; Calvin said 'it opened the door to all the treasures in the Scriptures'; Luther pronounced it 'The chief book of the New Testament and the purest gospel'; and Melanchthon, in order to become thoroughly acquainted with it, copied it twice with his own hand. Godet described it as 'the cathedral of the Christian faith'.

## Purpose

This letter answers the query of the ages: 'How should man be just with (or before) God?' (Job 9: 2) No one can be just who is not adjusted with his maker. This epistle reveals and expounds God's way of justification. Its key verses are 1: 16, 17. These two verses could be considered as the text, and all the rest of the letter as the sermon.

## Analysis

It is in two sections. Like a wise preacher, Paul first gives the doctrine (cc. 1 to 11), then makes the application (cc. 12 to 16). The first section is subdivided into nine divisions.

## DOCTRINAL

### Justification by faith revealed in the gospel (1: 1-17)

1 After opening greetings, Paul desires to visit Rome (i) to satisfy his own heart, (ii) to be the means of blessing to them, (iii) to discharge a debt, by preaching the gospel.
2 This gospel reveals God's methods of bestowing righteousness, God's way of justifying the sinner.
3 This is the basal text (vv.16, 17).

### The universal need of justification by faith (1: 18 to 3: 20)

1 All mankind shown to be in absolute need of God's justifying grace.
2 How the Gentiles got away from God, and the awful results that followed (1: 18-32).
3 C. 2 proves that the Jew stands equally in need of that same grace.
4 Justification by faith is only for those whose 'mouths have been stopped'.

### How we are justified (3: 21-31)

1 Its fountain, grace (v.24).
2 Its ground, blood (v.25 and 5: 9).
3 Its channel, faith (vv.28, 26, 22).
4 Its proof, resurrection of Christ (4: 25).
5 Its evidence, works (see James 2: 14-26).
(Note v.23 — All men are not sinners alike; yet all are alike sinners.)

### Justification by faith no new doctrine (c. 4)

1 Is not this doctrine new, a novel idea? By no means.
2 Abraham was justified by faith.
3 And David described the blessedness of the justified — a very important section.
(Note RV of v.19, where the negative is omitted, He deliberately faced the problem.)

### Blessings that follow justification (c. 5)

Peace (v.1), access (v.2), joy (v.2), glory in tribulation (v.3), love of God in heart (v.5).
(Note 1 V.5 — the first mention of Spirit in this epistle.
2 We are directed to Christ's work *for* us, before the Spirit's work *in* us.)

### Justification by faith and the question of sin (c. 6)

Justification by faith does not encourage continuance in sin; we have died to it.
(Note RV of v.2, 'We who died to sin'. For 'Old man' 20th Century Version gives 'old self'.)

### The struggles and the groans of the justified (c. 7)

Without doubt, the experience of a regenerate person; though many an awakened, but unconverted, one has a similar experience.
Here we witness battle in progress between our old nature and our new.

### Liberty and privileges for the justified (c. 8)

Here we have the promised land, flowing with milk and honey, for all to possess. What a contrast to the previous chapter!
This one begins with 'no condemnation', and ends with 'no separation'.

### Justification and the unbelieving Jew (cc. 9 to 11)

What about Israel? C. 9 is devoted to vindicating the liberty of God to mould his plans according to his fore-knowledge; c. 10, why Israel was rejected; c. 11, Israel's rejection is only partial, and not permanent.

## PRACTICAL

### The duties of the justified (cc. 12 to 16)

1 To God — to consecrate ourselves, with no conformity to the world (12: 1, 2).
2 To ourselves — not to be conceited (12: 3).
3 To the church — to use our gifts (12: 4-8).
4 To other Christians — to love, in varied ways (12: 9-13).
5 To the enemy — to 'avenge not', etc. (12: 14-21).
6 To the State — to 'Be subject' (13: 1-7).
7 To neighbours — to 'Owe no man anything' except love (13: 8-14).
8 To weak brother — to consider him (14: 1 to 15: 7).
9 To all — to observe the common courtesies of life (15: 8 to 16: 27).

# 46
# The First Epistle to the Corinthians

Key phrase: 'Our Lord'
Key verse: 1: 2
Theme: The Lordship of Christ

## The church
The church at Corinth was founded by Paul, as the result of eighteen months' labour there (1 Cor. 4: 15, with Acts c. 18).

## Origin of epistle
1 After Paul's departure, grave disorders broke out. During his three years' stay at Ephesus (Acts c. 19 and 20: 31) he must have rushed over to Corinth for a few days to put these abuses in order (first visit, Acts c. 18; 1 Corinthians and 2 Corinthians were written towards the close of the third year's ministry in Ephesus (1 Cor. 16: 8), and yet in 2 Corinthians 12: 14 and 2 Corinthians 13: 1, he speaks of paying his third visit).
2 On his return he wrote his first letter, now lost, (see 1 Cor. 5: 9, 11), thus making what we call the 'first letter', Paul's second, and the 'second' Paul's third.
3 The arrival and report of some members of a well-known family (1 Cor. 1: 11), and common reports from other travellers (1 Cor. 5: 1; 11: 18) prove that in spite of all his efforts, the sad disorders continued. Presently a reply to his first letter came, with fresh enquiries (1 Cor. 7: 1), and to answer these questions, as well as to unburden his soul further about the disorders, he wrote this letter.

## Clue and key
1 The clue to the message and understanding of this epistle is the mental, moral and spiritual condition of the Corinthians.
2 Though the members of the Corinthian church were chiefly drawn from the lower classes (1 Cor. 1: 26), they were not free from the peculiar tendency of the Greek to intellectual pride. 'Corinth was the rival of Athens. The Greeks were proud of their language, literature, learning and logic. Paul prepares this epistle to meet the Greek mind. He begins by renouncing wisdom (1 Cor. 1: 17; 2: 1; etc.) This epistle is throughout a rebuke to the princes of this world, confident in their worldly wisdom, but fools in God's sight. The world by wisdom knew not God (1 Cor. 1: 21). The natural man does not, cannot receive the things of the Spirit; the highest truths are veiled to him (1 Cor. 2: 14)' (Dr Pierson).

3 They were also addicted to immorality (1 Cor. 5: 1-11; 6: 15-18) and drunkenness (1 Cor. 11: 21), characteristic sins of their city.

## Tone
This epistle is distinctly an epistle of reproof. Even the doctrine it contains is by way of reproof and correction (see 1 Cor. 15: 12). It is intensely practical (even the glowing resurrection chapter is made an incentive to service), reproving and correcting abuses in the social and ecclesiastical life of the people; and though primarily intended only for the Christians at Corinth, the principles declared make it suitable and applicable to God's people of all time.

## Message
A careful study of the New Testament reveals that our Lord's full title — Lord Jesus Christ — is never given to him, except when the writer is seeking to declare and emphasise the Lordship of Christ. How significant, then, it is to find this title given to our Lord six times in the first ten verses (2, 3, 7, 8, 9, 10). The name 'Lord' is very prominent (1: 31; 2: 8, 16; 3: 20; 4: 4; 5: 4, 5; 6: 13; etc.). 'There is deep significance in this, for all the disorders that had crept into their lives had arisen through failure to recognize Jesus Christ as Lord.' Let us crown him Lord of our lives!

## Analysis
It falls naturally into two principal sections dealing with matters (1) reported to Paul (2) enquired of Paul.

## INTRODUCTION

(1: 1-9)
Address, greeting and thanksgiving.

## REPORTED TO PAUL

**1 Church Disorders (1: 10 to 4: 21)**
1 Party division denounced (1: 10-18).
2 Worldly wisdom denounced (1: 19 to 2: 16).
3 The true ministry —
Hindrances (3: 1-4).
Source of success (3: 5-10).
Two kinds (3: 11-23).
Our Master (4: 1-21).

**2 Social Irregularities (5: 1 to 6: 8)**
1 Immorality denounced (c. 5).
2 Want of brotherly love strongly rebuked (6: 1-8).

## ENQUIRED OF PAUL

**1 Social Irregularities (6: 9 to 10: 33)**
1 On marriage, celibacy and divorce (6: 9 to 7: 40).
2 On meat offered to idols (c. 8).
3 Paul on his authority and example (c. 9).
4 Lesson from Israel (10: 1-15).
5 Law of love in relation to eating and drinking (10: 16-33).

**2 Church Disorders (cc. 11 to 16: 4)**
1 Womanly modesty at church (11: 1-16).
2 Disorders at the Lord's table rebuked (11: 17-34).
3 Spiritual gifts (c. 12).
4 On love (c. 13).
5 Prophecy, the greatest gift (c. 14).
6 The grand resurrection chapter (c. 15).
7 'Concerning the collection' (16: 1-4).

## CONCLUSION

(16: 5-24)
Plans, personalities, salutations.

# 47
# The Second Epistle to the Corinthians

**Key words: Comfort, Ministry**
**Key verses: 1: 3, 4; 6: 4**
**Themes: 1 Comfort: its nature and bestowal**
**          2 Ministry: its message and performance**

## Circumstances

After writing the first epistle to the Corinthians, and sending it by the hand of Titus, Paul left Ephesus, his departure, no doubt, being hastened by the tumult (see Acts 19: 23-41). He slowly made his way to Troas (preaching en route) where he had arranged to meet Titus on his return from Corinth. Here Paul was much used of God. But the return of Titus was delayed. This greatly troubled Paul. So great was his anxiety to hear of the reception and result of his first letter, that, fearing the worst, he crossed the Aegean Sea, and went to meet him. Eventually they met at Philippi (2 Cor. 2: 12, 13; 7: 5, 6). Paul was probably ill in body, too (2 Cor. 1: 8-10).

## Purpose

From Titus, Paul learned that his first letter had served its purpose, both the church and the culprit being thoroughly repentant (2 Cor. 7: 7-16; 2: 1-11). But the same messenger informed him of a fresh peril — Judaising teachers, armed with letters of introduction from the church at Jerusalem, had arrived at Corinth, preaching another gospel, and denouncing the apostleship of Paul. The result of their labours was the rapid growth of a party hostile to him (3: 1-3; 4: 2; 10: 10; 11: 1-4, 12, 13). Therefore, he wrote this second epistle (1) to explain why he had not as yet been able to visit them (1: 15-24; 2: 1-3); (2) to praise them for obeying his first letter (7: 4, 15); (3) to urge the restoration of the repentant transgressor (2: 6-9); (4) to warn a few who were yet unrepentant (12: 21; 13: 2); (5) to warn them against the false teachers (11: 3, 4, 13); (6) to vindicate his apostleship (cc. 12 with 11); and to urge them to pay their promised contribution for the poor saints at Jerusalem (8: 10, 11).

## Revelation of Paul

This second epistle contains more of Paul's personal history than any other of his epistles. It is, in fact, a revelation of Paul himself. It certainly is a manifestation of the amazing depth and strength of his love, and the secret is 5: 14. It shows that he suffered from bodily weakness at times (1: 8-10; 12: 7-9); no wonder, when one remembers his labours, his sufferings and hardships (11: 23-33). Do not 10: 10 and 11: 6 give us a little knowledge of his personal appearance and speech? C. 12 reveals a secret Paul kept for fourteen years.

## Message

The epistle contains many glowing and brilliant metaphors (2: 15 [Twentieth Century Version]; 3: 3; 3: 18 RV; 4: 7; 5: 20, etc.) and most suggestive statements for preachers, but its special message is two-fold. The two words that are met with most frequently are 'comfort' and 'ministry', and the study of these words forms helpful Bible readings, besides giving the message of the book.

COMFORT — Source (1: 3); purpose (1: 4); compensations (1: 5); Christian duty (2: 7); how God sometimes comforts (7: 6, 7, 13); imperative command (13: 11).

MINISTRY — Satan has his (11: 15); God has his (6: 4); message (4: 5; 1: 19; 2: 12); a spiritual (3: 6), and glorious ministry (3: 8); leads to the transformation of character (3: 3); helps us not to faint (4: 1); is a ministry of reconciliation (5: 18); necessitates carefulness (6: 3).

## Points

This epistle is notable for many things. Often in the Old Testament God is spoken of as almighty, but he is so referred to only ten times in the New, nine of these being in Revelation, and the other in this epistle (2 Cor. 6: 18). One notable feature is that it provides us with the form of benediction now so general, with which most Christian gatherings are closed (see 2 Cor. 13: 14).

## Analysis

It is almost impossible to analyse this letter, as it is the least systematic of Paul's writings. It resembles an African river. For a time it flows smoothly on, and one is hopeful of a satisfactory analysis, then suddenly there comes a mighty cataract and a terrific upheaval, when the great depths of Paul's heart are broken up. However, the letter falls roughly into three sections.

## Explanation
### (cc. 1 to 7)

He explains the reason for his delay in visiting them; why he spoke so plainly and sternly in his first letter; why he was so concerned on their behalf; and gives an account of his sufferings.

## Exhortation
### (cc. 8, 9)

He exhorts them to a prompt fulfilment of their promise to contribute for the relief of the needy brethren in Jerusalem, especially as he had boasted to the Macedonian churches of that promise.

## Vindication
### (cc. 10 to 13)

A change in the apostle's tone can be detected in this section — there is sternness, and irony, as he vindicates his apostleship, and proves his right to their love and respect.

# 48
# The Epistle to the Galatians

Key word: Faith
Key verse: 3: 2
Theme: Christ, the deliverer from the law and mere externalism, leading into glorious liberty.

## Galatia

Galatia, a broad strip of country in Asia Minor, was inhabited by a mixed race, with Gauls predominating. These Gauls left their own country (now known as France) 300 years B.C., and after a successful military campaign, settled here, and gave their name to the land. Even today, travellers are struck with 'the fair hair and blue eyes that mark an affinity between the pastoral tribes of Galatia and the peasantry of western France'.

## Church

Here Paul, delayed by illness (4: 13) during his second missionary tour (Acts 16: 6), preached the gospel. It appears that the burden of his addresses was 'Christ crucified' (3: 1); that he was received as a heavenly messenger (4: 14); that he was able to establish a church (1: 6); and that the Galatians lavished their love upon him (4: 15).

## Purpose

1 But the Celtic temperament is very fickle, loving novelty and change, and when the Judaising teachers came that way, teaching salvation by works and the necessity of circumcision, etc., in unseemly haste (1: 6) they embraced these views.
2 Paul heard of their backslidden condition, and so urgent did the matter seem, that, no amanuensis being near, he did what he did not usually do, he wrote the whole of the epistle himself (6: 11).

## Peculiarities

1 Note: there is an unusual tone of severity about this epistle. Paul begins without a word of praise or thanksgiving, which is most unusual with him. There is no request for prayer — how could they, being themselves backsliders, pray for others?
2 This epistle has done more than any other book of the New Testament for the emancipation of the Christian from Judaism, Romanism, ritualism, and every other form of externalism that has ever threatened the freedom and spirituality of the gospel.
3 This was Luther's favourite epistle, and played a very important part in the glorious Reformation under the reformers.
4 Galatians 'takes up controversially what Romans puts systematically'; and it shows the Lord Jesus as the deliverer.
5 The doctrine of justification by faith is stated here more emphatically than in any other of Paul's writings. Note the emphasis Paul places on the inward and spiritual nature of the Christian faith in contrast to the mere externalism of the other '-isms' (see 1: 16; 2: 20; 4: 6, 19).

## Analysis

This epistle is in four parts, which are subdivided into eleven sections, as follows:

| Introduction | Paul's Apostolic Authority | Defence and exposition of salvation and sanctification by faith alone | | | Conclusion |
|---|---|---|---|---|---|

### Introduction

**Paul's cool**

### Greeting
(1: 1-5)
With the barest salutation, Paul introduces the atonement, a truth once so dear to them, but now practically rejected by them.

**Paul's stern**

### Reproof
(1: 6-9)
He expresses his great surprise that they should so soon have accepted another gospel, which was no gospel at all.

### Paul's Apostolic Authority

**Paul's gospel received by direct**

### Revelation
(1: 10-24)
Here he proves that he received his gospel direct from the Lord himself, in the wilds of Arabia.

**With Peter and others, great**

### Contention
(2: 1-15)
Paul herein shows how he had always resisted the Judaisers, even going to the length of openly correcting Peter.

### Defence and exposition of salvation and sanctification by faith alone

### Justification
by faith alone
(2: 16-19)
As Jews, they had experienced the inability of the law to save. But what the law could not do, grace had done. Justification is by faith, and faith alone.

### Divine union
by faith
(2: 20, 21)
Faith not only leads us into justification, but also into identification with Christ, in his death and resurrection, and union of the soul with the Lord.

### Reception of the Spirit
by faith
(3: 1-22)
But we are not only justified, we also receive the sanctifying Spirit. So the justified state leads to a state of sanctification, and that by faith.

### Sonship
through faith
(3: 23 to 4: 31)
Not only are we justified by faith, but we also become the children of God, through faith, and are enabled to realize our sonship by the indwelling Spirit.

### Liberty
through faith
(c. 5)
Christ leads into glorious freedom — a liberty we must preserve at all cost. But liberty does not mean license.

### Conclusion

### Service
in compassion and faith
(6: 1-10)
We must deal compassionately and sympathetically with each other, especially the erring ones.

### Conclusion
(6: 11-18)
A magnificent conclusion! Note RV rendering of v. 17 — 'I bear branded on my body . . .'

# 49
# The Epistle to the Ephesians

**Key phrase: The church**
**Key verses: 1: 22, 23; 5: 30**
**Theme: The church, the body of Christ**

## The church

Paul was the founder of the church at Ephesus. His first visit, in the spring of 54, was very brief, as he had to be in Jerusalem by a certain date, to complete a vow (Acts 18: 19-21), but afterward he spent three years of whole-hearted and intensely active service there (Acts 19: 8-10; 20: 31).

## The epistle

This epistle was written during Paul's first imprisonment at Rome, ten years after he had established the Ephesian church. It has been well said that 'this epistle surpasses all others in sublimity of style, and is pre-eminent, even amongst the apostle's writings, for the sustained majesty of its theme, and for a certain spiritual splendour, both in conception and in language'. Dr Pierson has called it 'Paul's third heaven epistle', for in it 'he soars from the depths of ruin to the heights of redemption'. It has also been called 'the alps of the New Testament, for here we are bidden by God to mount, step by step, until we reach the highest possible point where man can stand, even the presence of God himself'.

## Its teaching

Its distinctive teaching is concerning the church as the body of Christ, and believers as members of that sacred body. It proves that the Father not only prepared a body for the Lord Jesus to suffer in, but also a body mystical, in which he should be glorified. As we have two epistles on justification (Romans and Galatians), so we have two concerning the church — this and Colossians. The latter pair, written at the same time, may at first sight seem alike; but on closer inspection, we find in Ephesians the emphasis laid upon the church as the body of Christ, while in Colossians, Christ as the head of the body is the prominent truth.

## Key words

1 This epistle abounds in key words — In Christ Jesus, etc. (1: 1, 6, 7, 11, 13; 2: 6, 10, 13, 21, 22; 4: 21); Walk (2: 2, 10; 4: 1, 17; 5: 2, 8, 15); Together (1: 10; 2: 5, 6, 21); Therefore (2: 19; 4: 1, 17; 5: 1, 7, 24); Wherefore (1: 15; 2: 11; 3: 13; 4: 8, 25; 5: 14, 17; 6: 13); According to (1: 5, 9, 11, 19; 2: 2; 3: 7, 11, 16, 20); In heavenly places (1: 3, 20; 2: 6; 3: 10); Riches (1: 7, 18; 2: 7; 3: 8, 16); Love (1: 4; 3: 17; 4: 2, 15, 16; 5: 2).

2 This epistle gives three distinct figures of the church of Christ: (1) Temple (2: 21, 22), (2) Human body (1: 22, 23; 4: 15), (3) Bride (5: 25-32), but that of the body is emphasised, and is the main teaching of Ephesians.

---

## DOCTRINAL SECTION (cc. 1 to 3)

### Greetings to members of his body (1: 1, 2)

'In Christ Jesus' (as the body is joined to the head) is one key phrase of this epistle. 'In' him we are and have all.

### Blessings for members of his body (1: 3-14)

These verses reveal the eternal counsels of God, to 'Gather together in one all things in Christ'. Verse 10 is significant. (Note nine 'alls' in this chapter.)

### Prayer on behalf of members of his body (1: 15-21)

There are two prayers in this epistle, here, and in 3: 14-21. In the first, he prays they may have *light to know*, and in the second, *strength to know*.

### Christ the head of his body, the church (1: 22, 23)

What exalted teaching! Jesus the head of a new order, of a new body, the church. (More fully developed in Colossians.)

### How we are fitted to be members of his body (2: 1-10)

God's work seen in forming the body: the members were dead in sins, but had been forgiven, quickened, seated with Christ.

### A blessed association is membership of his body (2: 11-22)

'Remember' — 'where the sweetness of forgiveness is, there is the sadness of remembrance.' (Compare 2: 19 with 1 Peter 2: 11.)

### Gentiles have a portion and place in his body (c. 3)

Teaching concerning the Gentiles was specially revealed to Paul; the preaching of it was the cause of his imprisonment (see v.1).

---

## PRACTICAL SECTION (cc. 4 to 6)

### The unity of his body (4: 1-3)

Members of his body must abstain from anything that breaks unity; do all they can to foster and strengthen it.

### The unifying powers of his body (4: 4-6)

1 The unifying powers of the body are here demonstrated.
2 God is not only 'above all' and 'through all' but 'in you all'.

### The edifying of his body (4: 7-16)

1 Various gifts edify the body.
2 The word 'perfecting' is remarkable; it means 'repairing', 'making good the damage'.

### The duties of members of his body (4: 17 to 6: 24)

Concerning: one's walk (4: 17 to 5: 20); one's home life (5: 21 to 6: 4); one's employment (6: 5-9); one's 'warfare' (6: 10-24).

# 50
# The Epistle to the Philippians

Key word: All
Key verses: 4: 1-3
Theme: Christian unity to be maintained at all cost

## The epistle
1 This epistle ought to be greatly valued by Europeans, because it was written to the first church founded in Europe (Acts 16: 9-40).
2 A bishop of Durham calls this 'one of the fairest and dearest regions of the book of God'. Though not one of the most remarkable or deepest, it is yet one of the sweetest of Paul's writings. It is more in the nature of a love letter to the Philippians, who excelled all others in devoted attachment to Paul. Through this letter we get a glimpse into the apostle's heart.

## Notable points
(a) There is not a solitary quotation from the Old Testament scriptures in it.
(b) The word 'joy' or 'rejoice' is found in every chapter (1: 4, 18, 25, 26; 2: 2, 16, 18; 3: 1, 3; 4: 1, 4, 10).
(c) Note the recurrence of the word 'mind' (1: 27; 2: 2, 3, 5; 3: 15, 19; 4: 2, 7).
(d) Only three times is the Spirit mentioned, but how significant is each passage: (1) Supply of the Spirit (1: 19); (2) Fellowship of the Spirit (2: 1); (3) Worship by the Spirit (3: 3).
(e) Dr Pierson calls this epistle 'the Disciple's balance sheet', for here the apostle shows the renunciations and compensations of a disciple, and the excess in his favour (3: 4-14).
(f) This epistle contains less of censure, and more of praise, than any other.

## The church
The Philippian church was noted for its generosity. Repeatedly it had ministered to the wants of Paul (4: 15, 16). Hearing of the apostle's imprisonment in Rome, they sent help again by the hands of Epaphroditus (4: 10, 18) who, however, was smitten down on his arrival by an almost fatal illness. Somehow news of this illness had reached the Philippians, to their consternation; and on his recovery, Epaphroditus was anxious to reassure them in person (2: 25-28), so Paul wrote this letter for him to take.

## Object
1 The object of this letter was two-fold. First, to thank them for their generous gift. But there was a more serious purpose. Through Epaphroditus, the apostle had learned that dissension had broken out, threatening the peace and usefulness of the church.
2 Women right from the first had an important place in that church. Two of the leading women had fallen out (4: 2). The subject of dissension was probably some phase of the doctrine of Christian perfection — note the prominence given to this truth. Apparently the church had taken sides, and had split in two.
3 Observe how Paul seeks to bring unity again. He refuses to recognise two parties, hence is constantly using the word 'all': (if we pencil-mark each 'all', we will be surprised). He did not lecture the women: indeed he wisely makes no reference to them until the letter is nearly ended. Instead, he seeks to fill their minds with our Lord's greatness, but also his lowliness, meekness, and long-suffering. And he offers very pressing exhortations to unity. (Ponder 1: 27; 2: 1, 2, 3; 3: 15, 16; 4: 2).
4 Sometimes it is thought that this epistle ought to have followed and not separated Ephesians and Colossians, with their wonderful church teaching; but on further reflection one can only be thankful it is where it is. Ephesians speaks of the church as the body of Christ, and the mystic unity existing between HIM and the church. This Philippian letter shows how that unity can be broken, or maintained.

| Salutation | Prayer | Christ Glorified | Christ's Humility | Warnings | Exhortations |
|---|---|---|---|---|---|
| **to all**<br>**(1: 1, 2)** | **for all**<br>**(1: 3-11)** | **through Paul's imprisonment — an encouragement to all**<br>**(1: 12-30)** | **an example to all**<br>**(c. 2)** | **for all**<br>**(c. 3)** | **for all**<br>**(4: 1-20)** |
| 1 Note how Paul goes out of his way to emphasise that he was writing to ALL<br>2 'At Philippi', but thank God, 'in Christ Jesus'. | Paul's prayers make an interesting study, always. Here he prays — 'With joy; for more love; (but not a blind love); that they might have good taste; might be sincere, and filled with fruits'. | His imprisonment led to wide dissemination of the gospel though many preached with unworthy motives. But Paul's love for the Lord (v.21), and their sufferings would glorify the Lord, provided they were united. | Pride being foe of unity, Paul sets humility of the Lord as example for them to copy (vv.1-5). Christ's seven-fold humiliation and exaltation (vv.6-11). The effect should be humility, lowliness of heart and mind, the cure for spiritual pride. | 1 Against false teachers (vv.1-3);<br>2 Against self-righteousness (vv.4-6);<br>3 Against absolute, in stead of progressive perfection (vv.7-14 with 1: 6, 9; 2: 12, 13);<br>4 Against false professors (vv.15-19). | To Unity (vv.1-3),<br>Rejoicing (v.4)<br>Self-control (v.5)<br>Peace of God (vv.6, 7)<br>Careful thought (v.8)<br>Contentment (with its source) (vv.11-14). |

### Greeting
**from all and to all**
**(4: 21-23)**

1 'Every saint' saluted.
2 'All saints' send salutation — even saints in Caesar's household.

# 51
# The Epistle to the Colossians

Key phrase: He is the head
Key verse: 2: 8
Theme: The supreme glory and dignity of Christ

## Heresy at Colosse

1 Paul had, as fellow prisoner in Rome, one by the name of Epaphras (Philem. 23). When this man was converted, we do not know — probably during Paul's three years' ministry at Ephesus. As it is quite clear that the apostle had not founded the Colossian church (see 1: 4, 7, 8; 2: 1), it is thought that Epaphras had done so (1: 7; 4: 12).

2 It was from Epaphras that Paul learned that heresy had broken out at Colosse. What its precise nature was is a matter of discussion, but, judging by the contents of the epistle, we conclude that it was a curious mixture of Judaism, gnosticism, and asceticism, with angel worship, etc. One form of this heresy has been thus described: 'Flesh is essentially evil, God is essentially holy; between the essentially holy and the essentially evil, there can be no communion. It is impossible, said the heresy, for the essentially holy to touch the essentially evil. There is an infinite gulf between the two, and the one cannot touch and be intimate with the other. The heresy then had to devise some means by which this gulf might be crossed, and by which the essentially holy God could come into communion with an essentially evil state in which mankind was dwelling. What did it do? It said that out of the essentially holy God there emanated a being slightly less holy, and then out of the second holy one, there emanated a third one less holy still, and then out of the third a fourth, and so on, with an increasing dilution of holiness, with divinity more and more impoverished, until one appeared (Jesus) who was so emptied of divinity, of holiness, so nearly like man, that he could touch man' (Jowett).

3 One thing is certain, as bishop Moule points out, 'It was a doctrine of God and of salvation which cast a cloud over the glory of Jesus Christ — it put Jesus Christ into the background.' This heresy, anyone can see, (1) destroyed the supreme lordship and sovereignty of Jesus Christ — it dethroned him, emptying him of divinity, and (2) it destroyed the supreme mediatorship of Christ, making him only one of a multitude of mediators.

## Purpose

One could profitably study this epistle by looking at its portrait of the church (in which the headship of Christ is emphasised, 1: 18; 2: 10, 19) of the Christian (1: 13, 14, etc.), and Christian worker (4: 7-13, etc.), but the chief object and purpose of the letter is to draw a faithful portrait of the Lord Jesus in all his dignity, deity, and glory.

## Analysis

The letter is in two main divisions, each of which is subdivided into three sections as follows:

---

## DOCTRINAL

**Thanksgivings on behalf of the Colossians (1: 1-8)**
1 Note, faith first exercised before love manifested (v.4).
2 In v.8 we have the only mention of the Holy Spirit in the epistle.

**Intercession on behalf of the Colossians (1: 9-14)**
1 Note 'to pray for you, and to desire' (v.9).
2 This prayer has no formal ending, but merges into 'a worshipping and enraptured confession of the glory of the Christ of God'.

**The supreme dignity, glory, and pre-eminence of the Lord Jesus, viewed from every standpoint (1: 15 to 2: 3)**
The heart of the epistle. In hushed, and awed mood, Paul gives a heart-moving, soul-subduing affirmation of the glory of the Lord Jesus. Christ is seen as 'all and in all' —
in DEITY — equality with God — 'image of God' (v.15), abode of fulness (1: 19; 2: 9), and firstborn (v.15), a title of dignity.
in CREATION — Christ is cause, head and goal of the created universe (v.16).
in PROVIDENCE — In v.17, he who by one creative act formed the universe, by continuous activity sustains it.

in CHURCH — In Ephesians we see what the body is to the head, in Colossians what the head is to the body (v.18). In Ephesians, emphasis is placed on the church as body, in Colossians on Christ as its head.
in REDEMPTION — (vv.20, 23) he is the redeemer, and his redemption has wide extent.
in GOSPEL MYSTERY — (vv.24-29) the mystery is 'Christ in you'.

## PRACTICAL

**Warnings against error and heresy (2: 4-23)**
They are warned against: enticing words (v.4); vain philosophy (v.8); ritualism (vv.16, 17); angel worship (v.18); and empty, vain self-humblings and self-denials (vv. 20-23).

**Union with Christ and its results (3: 1 to 4: 6)**
Joined to our risen Lord we must show:
1 Heavenly mindedness (vv.1-3);
2 Holy living in home, service, all the walks of life (3: 4 to 4: 6).

**Greetings to the Colossians (4: 7-18)**
What a rich assemblage of Christian workers we have here. (Note the peculiarities of each.)

# 52
# The First Epistle to the Thessalonians

**Key phrase: Wait for his Son**
**Key verse: 1: 10**
**Theme: The Coming of the Lord *for* his people**

### First of epistles
This was the first of Paul's epistles, written from Corinth, probably about the year A.D. 53.

### The church
The church at Thessalonica was planted by Paul in the course of his second missionary journey (Acts 17: 1-9), after his memorable visit to Philippi. Though Paul could have spent only about a month there, yet he laboured so strenuously and faithfully, that a church was not only founded, but firmly established. Like the man in Acts 3: 7-9, these young converts dispensed with the customary crawling and creeping stage, walking briskly right away; and they made such rapid growth that the apostle could immediately begin to feed them with strong meat, *i.e.*, election (1: 4); Holy Spirit (1: 6); Trinity (1: 1, 6); Second coming of Christ (1: 10), Holiness (4: 1-3): truths and doctrines now considered suitable only for those who have been long on the heavenly way.

### Purpose of epistle
1 By chapter 3: 6-8, we learn that this first epistle was written on the return of Timothy, whom Paul had sent from Athens (3: 1, 2). He was greatly cheered by the report of their vigorous and healthy state, but hastened to correct some erroneous views they held concerning the Lord's coming. For instance, they were in sorrow concerning some who had died, thinking that they would have no part in the glory of the second advent of the Lord; and others were so overwhelmed by the thought of the imminence of the Lord's return that they had ceased to work (4: 13-18; and vv.11, 12).
2 The teaching concerning our Lord's coming *for* his own was not known until the Lord revealed it to Paul (note 'by the word of the Lord' 4: 15).
3 Our Lord's coming is mentioned 318 times in the 260 chapters of the New Testament, occupying one in every twenty verses from Matthew to Revelation. Surely this should be sufficient to show its importance.

### Analysis
This short epistle is in five sections, four of which end with statements concerning Christ's coming, which admirably sum up previous teaching.

---

## THE LORD'S COMING

---

### An inspiring hope
**for the young convert — Conversion and the second advent (c. 1)**
1 Salutation (v.1);
2 Thanksgiving because of their splendid service, patience of hope, election, acceptance of the gospel, noble example, activity in preaching (vv.2-8);
3 In their conversion they turned: to God from idols (not from idols to God); to a life of service; to a life of expectancy, waiting for their Lord (vv.9, 10).

### An encouraging hope
**for the faithful servant — Service and the second advent (c. 2)**
A remarkable summary of the nature of Paul's service: it was — not in vain (v.1); bold in spite of opposition (v.2); frank and open (v.3); only for God's glory (vv.4-6); gentle (vv.7-9); backed up by holy living (vv.10-12); successful (vv.13-18). His greatest reward at the coming, next to seeing the Lord himself, would be sight of his converts sharing that event (vv.19, 20).

### A purifying hope
**for the believer — Purity of life and the second advent (3: 1 to 4: 12)**
1 Paul's anxiety (3: 1-4).
2 He could not live if they did not stand fast (v.8).
3 The coming an incentive to holiness (3: 13); a consistent walk (4: 1); purity (4: 3-8); brotherly love (4: 9, 10).
4 Looking for his glorious appearing, does not mean idleness (4: 11, 12).

### A comforting hope
**for the bereaved — Bereavement and the second advent (4: 13-18)**
Our loved ones who have died in him shall rise first. They will accompany our Lord as he comes for us.

Note. 'I shall go to him but he shall not return to me,' was all broken-hearted David could utter concerning his dead child (2 Sam. 12: 23); we who look for a Saviour, can say more, since 'them also which sleep in Jesus, will God bring with him'. Our loved ones will come to us.

### A rousing hope
**for the sleepy Christian — Alertness and the second advent (c. 5)**
1 Our Lord's coming will be 'as a thief in the night', swiftly, quietly, suddenly, unexpectedly.
2 But he will not come 'as a thief in the night' to those who look for him, for we 'are not in the darkness' (see v.4); and he will not surprise us, for we are expecting him.
3 This necessitates watchfulness.

# 53
# The Second Epistle to the Thessalonians

Key phrase: Day of the Lord
Key verses: 1: 7, 8
Theme: The Coming of the Lord *with* his people

## Why this epistle was written

Not very long after writing and forwarding his first letter to the Christians at Thessalonica, Paul found it necessary to write again. The reason for this was that it had been reported to him that, owing to a forged letter and a false verbal message, both supposed to have come from the apostle, with imaginary revelations of the Spirit (2: 2) given through some member or members of the Thessalonian church, they were distressed at the thought that they were now passing through the great tribulation, that the great and dreadful 'day of the Lord' had come.

## Teaching of the epistle

1 In this epistle, he sets their minds at rest by declaring that certain events must take place before the 'day of the Lord' will be ushered in: (1) A great falling away from the faith. (2) The coming of Christ *for* his people. (3) The coming into public view of the 'man of sin', and his open and awful campaign against the Lord. (4) Then the coming of the Lord with his people in terrible judgment. (See 2: 1-4 RV).
2 In the first letter, Paul taught that the saints who had fallen asleep in Christ would share the coming of the Lord; in his second he shows that the saints who are alive shall not be overtaken by the judgments of the 'day of the Lord'; in his first, he taught the Lord's coming would be sudden, but in the second, he points out that 'sudden' does not mean 'immediate'.

---

## THE COMING OF THE LORD

### A comfort to the persecuted. Persecution and the Lord's coming (1: 1-7)

1 Salutation (vv.1, 2).
2 Commendation (vv.3, 4). If we look we shall often find something to commend in those whom we denounce or reprove.
3 Inspiration (vv.4-7). The fact of the Lord's second advent:
(a) Inspired them to noble piety, growth in faith, deepening of love (v.3);
(b) Inspired them to great patience and trustfulness in persecution (v.4).
(c) For on his arrival glaring wrongs would be righted and vengeance meted out to all their oppressors (vv.5-7).

### A terror to the unconverted. The impenitent and the Lord's coming (1: 7-12)

1 These verses destroy the view that he will not come until the world is converted.
2 The world has never seen our Lord Jesus since it crucified him [like Joash (2 Chron. cc. 22, 23), he is hidden in the sanctuary]: now he will be made known to the whole world.
3 A vivid contrast with 1 Thess. 4: 14-18: there he comes attended by one angel, here by many; then seen only by his own, here by all (Rev. 1: 7); then 'for', now 'with' his saints (Jude v.14); then he came for a peaceable object, now for judgment (Jude v.15).

### The coming of the Lord for his people leads to the revealing of the 'man of sin'; the coming with his people means the 'man of sin's' destruction (2: 1-12)

1 It is important to note the RV rendering of vv.1, 2 to understand this chapter.
2 One of the most important prophecies in the New Testament — the Pauline prediction of antichrist.
3 'Man of sin' represents Hebrew for 'a man of eminent wickedness'.
4 Many hold that the 'man of sin' has already been revealed in the Papacy. While there are remarkable points here which harmonise with a just description of the Papacy, we cannot but conclude that he is yet to come.

Note 'The sin of man has its final outcome and fruition in the man of sin.' — 'Not until the Lord has caught up his own will the lawless one come into public view.' (Mauro). 'The mystery of godliness is God humbling himself to become man; the mystery of iniquity is man exalting himself to become God.' (A. J. Gordon)

### The delay of the Lord's coming means unique opportunities for service (2: 13 to 3: 18)

1 With what relief Paul turned from this awful subject to the believers (2: 13, 14).
2 Our Lord's delay gives unique opportunities — of loyalty to him (2: 15); of evangelising the world (3: 1); of praying for his servants (3: 1, 2); of patient waiting for him (3: 5); of living the separated life (3: 6-14); of tenderness towards the erring (3: 15).

# 54
# The First Epistle to Timothy

**Key phrase: 'How thou oughtest to behave'**
**Key verse: 3: 15**
**Theme: Designed to accomplish (1 Tim. 4: 12)**

## Timothy
Timothy was the son of a Greek father and a Jewish mother. He was converted at the age of fifteen, during Paul's ministry at Lystra (Acts c. 14; 1 Tim. 1: 2). Seven years afterwards he had so advanced in grace that he was 'well reported', and became Paul's companion (Acts c. 16), and there then began one of those beautiful friendships between an older and a younger man, which are usually so helpful to both (Phil. 2: 22).

## Circumstances
Immediately on his release from his first imprisonment before he visited Spain (Rom. 15: 24; Philem. v.22), Paul probably visited Macedonia, Ephesus, etc. Not being able to stay long at Ephesus, he left Timothy to take charge of the work. This parting was a sore trial to Timothy (1 Tim. 1: 3; 2 Tim. 1: 4). To encourage and instruct Timothy (who was sensitive, timid, and not strong 5: 23), Paul wrote and forwarded this letter from Corinth.

## Character
The two letters to Timothy and the one to Titus are known as Pastoral epistles. They were addressed to individuals, and not to congregations. Paul was about seventy when he wrote them, consequently we have in them the farewell words of the great apostle to ministers and Christian workers. In them we have the mellow wisdom of old age. All Christian workers have, for centuries, found these letters a source of encouragement and help. One prominent minister declared that he read them every Sabbath evening for his own soul's welfare.

## Peculiarities
There are several phrases found only in these Pastoral epistles. (1) 'God my Saviour', a phrase common enough in the Old Testament, with one exception (Luke 1: 47) is found in the New Testament only in the Pastoral epistles (1 Tim. 1: 1; 2: 3; 4: 10; Titus 1: 3; 2: 10, 13; 3: 4). (2) 'Godliness' is another expression confined entirely to these letters, with the exception of 2 Peter 1: 3, 6, 7; 3: 11 (1 Tim. 2: 2, 10; 3: 16; 4: 7, 8; 6: 3, 5, 6, 11; 2 Tim. 3: 5; Titus 1: 1). (3) 'Sound' (healthful, RV), a medical metaphor Paul probably borrowed from Luke, the beloved physician, is found only here, a sound 'mind' (2 Tim. 1: 7); words (2 Tim. 1: 13); doctrine (1 Tim. 1: 10; 2 Tim. 4: 3; Titus 1: 9; 2: 1); faith (Titus 1: 13); speech (Titus 2: 8). (4) 'Man of God', often met with in the Old Testament is found twice in the New Testament and only in the Pastoral epistles (1 Tim. 6: 11; 2 Tim. 3: 17). (5) Remembering Timothy's sensitiveness, and the meaning of 'mercy' (see Luke 10: 37; Gen. 39: 21), it is most suggestive to find, only in the Pastoral epistles, that 'mercy' is added to the usual couplet of 'grace and peace' (see 1 Tim. 1: 2; 2 Tim. 1: 2; Titus 1: 4; and the beginnings of other epistles). (6) Only in the Pastoral epistles do we find the 'faithful sayings' — Christian household proverbs (1 Tim. 1: 15; 3: 1; 4: 9, 10; 2 Tim. 2: 11-13; Titus 3: 8).

## Striking RV renderings
There are several striking renderings in the RV of this epistle: (1) 'Gospel of the glory' (1: 11), suggesting, not what the gospel is, but what it is about. (2) 'His longsuffering' 1: 16) — he gives the necessary grace, and enables us to suffer long and patiently. (3) 'Which thou hast followed until now' (4: 6). (4) 'Ready to sympathise' (6: 18 margin). (5) The finest definition of eternal life is 6: 19 — 'the life which is life indeed'.

## Analysis
The purpose of the epistle is admirably given in 1 Timothy 3: 15, and the whole of the contents is designed to enable the young worker to rise to the height of 1 Timothy 4: 12.

---

On the imperative need of
## Sound doctrine
(c. 1)
1 Introduction (vv.1, 2),
2 Why left (vv.3, 4),
3 Practical godliness (vv.5, 6),
4 The Law — its use and abuse (vv.7-11),
5 Personal testimony (vv.13-17),
6 A solemn charge (vv.18-20).

On the nature and order of
## Public prayer
(2: 1-8)
1 What to pray for (vv.1-3),
2 How to pray (v.8),
3 God's pleasure (v.3), desire (v.4), provision (vv.5-7), condition (4: 10).

On the qualifications necessary for
## Spiritual oversight
(2: 9 to 3: 16)
1 The scope of the ministry, and adornment of women (2: 9-15);
2 Qualifications necessary: to be irreproachable in family life (3: 2, 4, 5, 11, 12); in personal life (3: 2, 3, 6, 8); in public life (3: 7); in spiritual belief (3: 9).

The Christian worker's
## Spiritual duties
(cc. 4-6)
1 To warn others (4: 1-6);
2 To exercise oneself (4: 7, 8, 9-16);
3 How to treat others (c. 5);
4 Duty of servants (6: 1, 2);
5 Sundry exhortations (6: 3-21).

# 55
# The Second Epistle to Timothy

**Key word: Ashamed**
**Key verses: 1: 8, 12, 16; 2: 15**
**Theme: Loyalty to the Lord and truth, in view of persecution and apostasy**

## Paul's second imprisonment
After writing his first epistle to Timothy, Paul left Corinth, and set sail with Titus for Crete, where he left him to set the church in order (Titus 1: 5). On returning to the mainland, he wrote to Titus. On his way to Nicopolis, where he intended to winter (Titus 3: 12), Trophimus was left at Miletum sick, and Erastus at Corinth (2 Tim. 4: 20). Probably, whilst at Nicopolis, he rushed over on a short visit to Troas, but was arrested in the house of Carpus, and hurried to Rome. His arrest was so sudden that he had no time to gather up his precious books and parchments, or even to wrap his cloak around him (2 Tim. 4: 13). This second imprisonment was very different from the former one. (1) Then he had his own hired house, now he is kept in close confinement; (2) then he was accessible to all, now, even Onesiphorus could only find him with difficulty and at great risk (1: 16, 17); (3) then he was the centre of a large circle of friends, now, almost alone (4: 10-12); (4) then, he hoped for speedy liberation, now, he was expecting to die (4: 6).

## Paul's object in writing
Paul had appeared before Nero once, but his case had been adjourned (4: 16, 17). He expected to appear again in the winter, and wrote urging Timothy (who had been liberated, Heb. 13: 23), to come at once with Mark and the things that were left, (4: 9, 11, 13, 21). But, uncertain whether Timothy would arrive in time (he did not, for the trial and death took place long before winter — in June), he desired to give a last warning as to heresies, and encouragement to zeal, courage, and patience.

## Characteristics of epistle
This was the last epistle ever written by Paul. The personal nature of the epistle is remarkable, for there are references to twenty-three individuals, and one of them (Claudia) is believed to have been a British princess. Its style is abrupt, without plan or method, strongly emotional, with a vivid remembrance of the past, and anxious thoughts for the future. Paul, like his beloved Lord, though bearing the burden of loneliness, and the consciousness of approaching death, forgot himself in thoughts of others. A Bishop of Durham writes: 'I have often found it difficult deliberately to read these short chapters through, without finding something like a mist gathering in the eyes. The writer's heart beats in the writing.' Only in this epistle are we informed of the names of Timothy's relatives, and Moses' opponents. (See 1: 5; 3: 8).

## Some striking RV renderings
(1) Stir into flame (1: 6). (2) I know him (1: 12). (3) The good deposit (1: 14). (4) Be strengthened (2: 1). (5) Take thy part in suffering (2: 3). (6) Remember Jesus Christ (2: 8). (7) Handling aright (2: 15). (8) I have fought *the* good fight (4: 7).

## Five objects of love
(1) Money (1 Tim. 6: 10). (2) Self (2 Tim. 3: 2). (3) Pleasure (2 Tim. 3: 4). (4) World (2 Tim. 4: 10). (5) The cure for all these is the fifth — his appearing (2 Tim. 4: 8).

| Loyalty to the Lord, his truth, and servants in spite of **Suffering** | Loyalty to the Lord in devoted **Service** | Loyalty to the Lord and his truth in spite of **Apostasy** | The Lord standing by his loyal servant in **Desertion** |
|---|---|---|---|
| (c. 1) | (c. 2) | (3: 1 to 4: 5) | (4: 6-22) |
| 1 Paul's preaching (v.1), prayers (v.3), service (v.3), desires (v.4), thoughts (v.5). 2 Timothy's early days (v.5), beloved by Paul (v.2), remembered by Paul (vv. 3, 5), desired by Paul (v.4). 3 Why even the most timid should not be ashamed of the gospel (vv. 6-14). 4 A sad statement (vv. 15-18). | Five miniature parables on Christian service: restored invalid (v.1), faithful steward (v.2), hardy soldier (vv.3, 4), an athlete (v.5), a farmer (v.6). 2 The Christian worker's chief — remembrance (v.8), encouragement (v.9), support (v.13), study (v.15). 3 The unmoved foundation (vv.16-19). 4 The great house and its vessels (vv.20-22). 5 The power of gentleness (vv.23-26). | 1 A saddening catalogue of twentieth century vices (3: 1-9). 2 The holy scriptures (3: 10-17). 3 Two things Timothy knew: The book of Paul's life and character (v.10); The inspired book of God (v.15). 4 What a Christian preacher must do in perilous times (4: 1-6). (Note in Paul — ready for Service (Rom. 1: 15), ready for Suffering (Acts 21: 13), ready for Sacrifice (2 Tim. 4: 6). | 1 Christian life under three metaphors: Paul speaks: as a Soldier, likening life to a fight. as an Athlete, likening life to a race. as a Trustee, likening life to a sacred trust (4: 7, 8). 2 Paul, the man, seen in his sigh over loneliness (vv.9-12, 21), desire for bodily comfort (vv. 13, 21), suffering through an enemy (vv.14, 15), his plaintive lament over lack of friendly support (v.16). 3 Paul, the saint seen in his exulting testimony concerning the Lord (v.17), bold witness for the Lord (v.17), confidence in the Lord (v.18). |

# 56
# The Epistle to Titus

Key phrase: Thyself a pattern
Key verses: 2: 7, 8, 15
Theme: God's ideal for the Christian church and Christian workers

## Writer

Without doubt Paul wrote this epistle. Some have thought that because of its strong emphasis on works (1: 16; 2: 7, 14; 3: 1, 8, 14), Paul did not write it; but 3: 5 is a sufficient answer to that objection. It was written about the same time, and at the same place as 1 Timothy.

## Titus

It is quite clear that Titus was one of Paul's converts (1: 4). He must have been converted in the early years of Paul's ministry, for he accompanied Paul and Barnabas to Jerusalem at the conclusion of their first missionary journey, seventeen years after Paul's conversion. (See Gal. 2: 1.) Titus differed from Timothy in many respects. Timothy had been brought up as a Jew, and was circumcised by Paul; Titus was a pure Gentile, and was not circumcised (Gal. 2: 3). He must have been older than Timothy in years and grace; and certainly was a much stronger man physically and morally, for Paul seems less anxious about the conduct of Titus, and the way others might treat him, than he was about Timothy.

## Cretans

Paul does not give the Cretans a very good character (1: 12, 13). 'The Cretans are said to have been a turbulent race — or rather a group of turbulent races — neither peaceable among themselves, nor very patient of foreign dominion. Previous to their conquest by the Romans in 67 B.C., they had been accustomed to democratic forms of government, and therefore would be likely to feel the change to the Roman yoke more acutely. For all these reasons, Paul must have known that he was charging Titus (in 3: 1) to give instructions which would be very unwelcome, even to the Cretan converts.' Recognising the difficulties, Paul, who had great faith in the wisdom and ability of Titus, and had entrusted to him delicate missions e.g. to the Corinthians (2 Cor. 2: 13; 7: 6, 7), on leaving Crete after a visit, left Titus to put things in order (1: 5).

## Notable points

1 This epistle contains two of the most comprehensive statements of Christian truth to be found in the New Testament (2: 11-14; 3: 4-7).
2 The only time Paul calls himself a 'bondman of God' is in this epistle (see 1:1 RV).
3 Paul is the only New Testament writer who quotes from heathen writers. He does so three times: (1) in this epistle (1: 12), (2) in Acts 17: 28, and (3) in 1 Corinthians 15: 33.
4 This epistle enables us to see that Christ's personal and pre-millenial coming, of which Paul wrote so fully to the Thessalonians thirteen years before, was still to him in his old age a blessed hope (2: 13).

## Message

1 God's ideal for a church: Orderly organization, soundness in faith and morals, and practical works of piety and philanthropy.
2 God's ideal for a Christian worker: A love of order and method, a healthy and living orthodoxy, a sober mien, and chastened speech.

---

**Emphasis in this section is on church order**

## An orderly church
(c. 1; key 1:5)

1 Paul's loving and significant greeting (vv.1-4), (Note v.2, a striking contrast to the lying character of the Cretans, v.12).
2 Object in leaving Titus (v.5).
3 Qualifications for eldership (vv.6-9).
4 Unruly character of Cretans (vv.10-16).
(Note v.15: 'Unto the pure all things are pure'.)

**Emphasis in this section is on doctrine**

## A sound church
(c. 2; key 2: 1, 2, 7, 10)

1 A message for Titus (vv.1, 7, 8, 15); for the aged (vv.2, 3); for the young (vv.4-6); for the slaves (vv.9, 10).
2 Backed up by Paul's giving, in a sentence, all the gospel — past, present, and future (vv.11-14).

**Emphasis in this section is on works**

## A practical church
(c. 3; key 3: 1, 8, 14)

1 Practical citizenship (v.1).
2 Practical godliness (v.2).
3 A sad retrospect (v.3).
4 What led to our transformation (vv.4-7).
5 Need for practical piety (v.8).
6 What to avoid (v.9).
7 Whom to avoid (vv.10, 11).
8 Conclusion (vv.12-15).

# 57
# The Epistle to Philemon

Key word: Receive
Key verses: vv.12, 15, 17
Theme: The practice of Christian forgiveness enforced and illustrated

## Paul's private correspondence

Rev. Sir W. Robertson Nicoll wrote: 'If I were to covet any honour of authorship, it would be this: That some letters of mine might be found in the desks of my friends when their life struggle is ended.' One private letter of Paul's was so cherished. Of all Paul's *private* correspondence, Philemon is the only example that has been preserved. It is the briefest of all Paul's epistles, and a gem.

## The story in the epistle

A slave of Philemon (who was an important member of the church at Colosse), Onesimus by name, had absconded, and made his way to Rome, apparently with the aid of money stolen from his master. There he was providentially brought under the influence of Paul, was converted, and endeared himself to the apostle by his grateful and devoted service. But he was Philemon's lawful slave, and Paul could not think of retaining him permanently in his service, as he could not use the servant, and benefit by his labours, without the master's knowledge.

## Paul's problem and strategy

1 Paul wished to save the runaway slave from the severe and cruel punishment he merited according to Roman law. And he wanted to conciliate Philemon, without humiliating Onesimus; to commend the wrongdoer without extenuating his offence. How was this to be done?

2 Paul felt the slave must not encounter his outraged master alone; he secured a mediator in Tychicus, who was on his way to Colosse. Then he wrote this personal letter to Philemon, for Onesimus to take with him, a letter which is a model of tact and courtesy. Finally, to make it more difficult for Philemon *not* to pardon and restore the culprit, he commends him to the whole church (see Col. 4: 9).

## The epistle is of value

1 As a revelation of Paul's character. We learn more accurately the real character of a man from his private letters than from his public correspondence. By a study of this brief epistle — sometimes called 'the courteous epistle' — we find, in private life as in public, the consistency of Paul's character — he is the same courteous, lovable, humble, holy, unselfish man.

2 As an example of Paul's tact and wisdom. It is a masterpiece, a model of graceful, tactful, delicate pleading.

(1) To touch a chord of tenderness in Philemon's heart, he mentions several times that he was a prisoner (vv.1, 9, etc.). (2) He cordially acknowledges Philemon's excellencies, making it difficult for him not to exercise them in forgiving Onesimus (vv.4-7). (3) He delays mention of the name of Onesimus, until he had thus carefully paved the way. (4) He refuses to command with the authority of an apostle, pleading as a bosom friend (vv.8-10). He earnestly entreats (note 'beseech'), referring to Onesimus as 'my son' (v.10) and assuming Philemon would do as asked (v.21). (6) He frankly acknowledges the wrong done (v.11), promising to make good any loss (vv.18, 19). (7) Though once 'unprofitable' (v.11), Paul could vouch for a thorough change in Onesimus, and guarantee it (v.13). (8) He plays genially upon words (vv.2, 11), touching upon the providential aspect of the question (v.15). (9) He chooses words carefully. He says 'departed' not 'fled' or 'escaped', using no word that might awaken resentment in the master, and describing not the quality of the servant's act, but simply its external aspect. 'For a season' — a short while (v.15). (10) He mentions his hope of soon being liberated and seeing Philemon. How could he face Paul if he did not do as requested?

3 As an illustration of the gospel method of social reform. This epistle has been appealed to as furnishing support or apology for slavery. Could slavery exist long if verses 16, 17 were put into practice? It is a good illustration of the reforming influence of the gospel, which seeks to gain its end by persuasion, rather than compulsion; by gentleness, rather than by dynamite. It seeks to overthrow by undermining.

4 As an analogy of our redemption. 'The sinner is God's property, and he has not only run away from his master, but robbed him. The Law affords him no right of asylum, but grace concedes him the right of appeal. He flees for refuge to Jesus, whom God counts as partner. In him he is begotten anew, as a son, and finds both an intercessor and a father; he returns to God, and is received, not as a slave, but as Christ himself, and all the debt is put to Christ's account.'

## Key word and analysis

1 The letter's key word is 'receive'. Note how in vv.12, 15, 17 Paul strikes a louder note and a higher key each time he repeats it.

2 It falls naturally into four divisons:

| 1 Greeting (vv.1-3), | 2 Splendid character of Philemon commended (vv.4-7), | 3 Intercession for Onesimus (vv.8-21), | 4 Salutation and conclusion (vv.22-25). |

# 58
# The Epistle to the Hebrews

Key word: Better
Key verses: 1: 4; 8: 6
Theme: The cure for faintheartedness and backsliding is a right conception of the glory and work of Christ.

## Authorship

The writer of this epistle is uncertain. Eusebius tells us that Pantaenus of Alexandria (second century) assigned the authorship to Paul; Tertullian of Carthage (third century) declared Barnabas was the writer; Luther thought that Apollos had written it; Dr Campbell Morgan thought it bears traces of Paul's thinking and Luke's writing; and Dr Scofield believed that we have preserved in this epistle some of Paul's synagogue addresses. It must have been written about A.D. 64, as the Temple is referred to as still standing.

## Object

Owing to bitter persecution, the Jewish Christians were beginning to think they had lost everything (altar, priests, etc.) by espousing the cause of Christ. They had begun to undervalue Christian privileges, were getting absorbed with their sufferings, and were generally in a backslidden condition. The apostle (for no doubt Paul wrote it) sent this letter to rectify these errors.

## Skill

Note the writer's skill in dealing with these despondent and despairing Christians. (1) First he fills their minds with the glory of the person, and the grandeur of the work of the Lord Jesus; (2) he shows that, instead of losing all, they had gained all (note 'we have' in 4: 14; 6: 19; 8: 1; 10: 34; 13: 10, 14), and their Christianity was superior to Judaism; (3) and then he shows they had not yet suffered as much as others. Coleridge has beautifully pointed out that, while the Roman epistle proved the *necessity* of the Christian religion, the object of Hebrews was to prove the *superiority* of the Christian religion; and this the writer does, not by slighting the old, but by showing the new as the fulfilment of the old. They had good things in the old system, but they now have everything 'better'. This epistle has been called 'the Fifth Gospel' — the other four speak of Christ's work on earth, this speaks of that, but also of his work in heaven.

## Topical study

No book lends itself so readily for topical study, as follows: (a) Perfect (2: 10; 5: 9, 14 RV margin; 7: 11, 19, 28 RV; 9: 9, 11; 10: 14; 11: 40; 12: 2 RV). (b) Heavenly (1: 10; 3: 1; 4: 14; 6: 4; 7: 26; 8: 1, 5; 9: 23, 24; 10: 34; 11: 16; 12: 22, 23, 25, 26). (c) Eternal (1: 8; 5: 6, 9; 6: 20; 7: 17, 21, 24, 28; 9: 12, 14, 15; 13: 8, 20, 21). (d) Sat down (1: 3; 8: 1; 10: 11, 12; 12: 2). (e) Once (7: 27; 9: 12, 26, 27, 28; 10: 2, 10). (f) Better (1: 4; 6: 9; 7: 7, 19, 22; 8: 6; 9: 23; 10: 34; 11: 6, 35, 40; 12: 24).

## THE ARGUMENT:
### the glory of the person and work of Christ (1: 1 to 10: 18)

**The Lord Jesus, greater than prophets (1: 1-3)**

1 The prophets were great, the son is greater, because while God spake 'by' the prophets, he speaks 'in' his son — God's last word.
2 Observe the phrase 'sat down' in v.3 — one of the characteristic utterances of Hebrews suggesting a work perfectly finished.

**The Lord Jesus, greater than angels (1: 4 to 2: 18)**

1 Angels are great but the Lord Jesus is greater, for he is son of God, begotten of God; and God never said to them, as to the Lord Jesus, 'Thy throne O God'.
2 'The oil of gladness above thy fellows', v.9 proves our Lord was not only 'a man of sorrows' but also 'the man of gladness'.

**The Lord Jesus, greater than Moses (c. 3)**

1 How great was Moses — but Jesus is greater: Moses, a faithful 'servant', Jesus a loyal 'son' over his own house.
2 This statement would fall with tremendous weight on Jews then, as indeed it does today.

**The Lord Jesus, greater than Joshua (4: 1-13)**

1 Joshua was great, yet failed; Jesus is greater — he alone can lead to real rest.
2 Is 'the Word of God' in v.12 the Lord Jesus? Certainly he is the Word of God, and 'alive and powerful', the all-wise and all-knowing one.

**The Lord Jesus, greater than Aaron, (4: 14 to 10: 18)**

Aaron and his successors were great, Jesus is better — sinless, while they were sinful (4: 15); priest after a higher order than Aaron's (5: 6); our fore-runner as Aaron never was (6: 20); Abraham acknowledged Melchisedec greater (7: 4); the order of Melchisedec is everlasting (7: 16. 17); Aaron served shadows, Jesus the realities (8: 1-5); as medium of a better covenant (8: 6-13); ministering in a better sanctuary (9: 1-25); and offering a better sacrifice (9: 25-28).

## THE APPLICATION: the life we should live
### because of his life and work (10: 19 to 13: 25)

1 Wisely, the writer did not leave application until the end, but repeatedly drove home his lesson (2: 1-4; 3: 7-19; 6: 1-12). Yet the application proper begins here, repeating the phrase, 'Let us'.

2 Let us: Be borne along (literal rendering) (6:1), Draw near (10: 19-22), Hold fast (10: 23), Consider one another (10: 24, 25), Persevere (10: 26 to 11: 40), Lay aside every weight and sin (12: 1), Run with patience (12: 1, 2), Endure manfully (12: 3-29), Let brotherly love continue (13: 1-4), Let conversation be without covetousness (13: 5), Go forth (13: 13), Offer the sacrifice of praise (13: 15).

# 59
# The Epistle of James

Key words: Faith (12 times), works (13 times)
Key verse: 2: 26
Theme: Faith shown by its works

## Author

1 Without doubt, James, the brother of our Lord, was its writer. Three men bearing the name of James are mentioned in the New Testament: (1) The son of Zebedee; (2) the son of Alphaeus; (3) James the Just, our Lord's brother, the writer of this letter.

2 He was bitterly opposed to our Lord during his earthly ministry, but was converted by a special and private interview with the risen one (1 Cor. 15: 7), became a man of prayer, was made bishop of the Jerusalem church (Acts 15: 13-21; Gal. 2: 9), and was slain by Jews, A.D. 62.

## Style

1 It was written by a Jew to Jewish Christians, and there is a great deal that is distinctly Jewish in its style and spirit.
2 One clue to the epistle is the character of James himself. He was stern and severe, much like the Old Testament prophets. His style is curt, bold, rapid; he was a wonderful man for metaphors (1: 6, 10, 17, 18, 21, 23; 5: 5).

## Time

By internal evidence, authorities are more and more coming to agree that we have in James the first of the New Testament epistles. It must have been written between A.D. 45 and A.D. 53. This is of vast importance. Many have imagined that James wrote his epistle to combat the Pauline view of justification by faith, as unfolded in Romans, whereas it was written some years before Romans.

## Purpose

1 Jewish Christians were passing through severe trials and temptations, and he writes to comfort and encourage them.
2 There were grave disorders in the early Jewish Christian assemblies, and he writes to correct them.
3 There was a tendency to divorce faith and works. 'A right strawy epistle,' says Luther, referring presumably to the 'stubble' of 1 Corinthians 3: 12 — 'Having no true evangelical character'. He was unable, through hasty views of the epistle, to reconcile it with the grand doctrine which he felt called upon to champion; but years afterwards he saw differently, that in fact James is really the complement to Paul. The proof that anyone is justified by faith is seen in his works.

## Contents

1 There is little doctrine here, but much of practice, and much of morals. James was exceedingly practical. He lived what he preached. This is a book of holy living.
2 Its key verse is 2: 26. It is, in reality, a very practical treatise on faith, its nature and work. It seems almost as fragmentary and disconnected as Proverbs, but on closer inspection beautiful order is discerned.

---

## Greeting

(1: 1)
Note humility — no reference to relationship to Jesus: James mentions Jesus only twice, but how reverently and devotedly. An attitude worthy of our attention, for familiarity usually breeds contempt.

## Faith tested and shown by our
## Temptations

(1: 2-21)
1 Count testing a glorious opportunity of proving faith (vv.2-4).
2 For wisdom to behave wisely in trial, when wronged, insulted, ask God (vv.5-11).
3 He who does not escape, but survives and conquers temptation, is blessed (v.12).

4 Temptations to evil do not come from God (vv.13-18).
5 Under trial, be slow to speak (vv.19-21).

## Faith shown by our
## Works

(1: 22 to 2: 26)
1 Be not deceived about God (v.16 RV), yourself (v.22), or religion (v.26).
2 'Respect of persons' is a breach of good manners, discourteous to the poor, and sin (2: 1-13).
3 2: 14-26 is the heart of the epistle, showing that living faith is always known by its fruits.

## Faith shown by our
## Words

(c. 3)
1 'It is quite apparent from this letter that there was a great deal of ill-considered, ill-natured, self-assertive, and violent speech among Jewish Christians; a great deal of angry debating and bitter strife.'
2 One proof of our justification is seen in our words — our speech reveals what, and whose, we are.

## Faith shown by lives of
## Unworldliness

(c. 4)
1 'The world is that order of things about us, or that spirit in us, which is blind and deaf to the value and reality of spiritual things, and careless to the will of God.'
2 Unworldliness is an infallible proof that we stand among the justified, that we have saving faith in Christ Jesus.
(Observe: 'Submit' to God before attempting to 'resist the devil'.)

## Faith shown by our
## patience under
## Cruel wrong

(5: 1-12)
1 Evidently many humble Christian Jews were oppressed by the wealthy, and defrauded of their hard earnings.
2 Faith in Christ and his coming will lead to patient sufferance of evils we cannot avoid.
(Observe: 'The just one' (v.6 RV).)

## Faith shown by our
## believing and effectual
## Prayers

(5: 13-20)
1 Tradition says James' knees were hard as a camel's through constant prayer.
2 What he practised he preached.
3 Note abrupt close — no leave-taking. It could not close more impressively.
(Observe: v.16, Weymouth version: 'Powerful is the heartfelt supplication of a righteous man.')

# 60
# The First Epistle of Peter

Key word: Suffering
Key verses: 3: 18; 4: 1
Theme: How we may be able to suffer patiently, joyously, and to the glory of God.

## For whom?

1 This letter was written by Peter towards the close of his life (A.D. 60), while he was staying at Babylon (5: 13), where a Christian church had been established, and was sent by the hand of Silas (5: 12), one of Paul's companions, now free for this work, as Paul was a prisoner.
2 It was intended principally, though not exclusively, for Hebrew Christians (Jews — 1: 1 RV; Gentiles — 2: 9, 10).

## Purpose

Evidently it was written for a two-fold purpose: First, many of the primitive Christians had begun to think that Paul and Peter held diverse views on the fundamentals of our Christian faith. It is thought that Peter wrote this epistle, and sent it, by the hand of Paul's companion, to the Asiatic churches planted by Paul, to demolish that error. It was also intended to strengthen and encourage the converted Jews who were passing through sore trial and bitter persecution, and thus perform the ministry our Lord had bade him exercise (see Luke 22: 31, 32).

## Peter transfigured

The portraits of Peter in the Gospels and his own writings are amazingly and gloriously different. In the former, Peter saw his Lord transfigured; in the latter, we see Peter transfigured by the boundless grace of God. In the former, we see Peter impetuous, courageous, restless, buoyant, quick to meet personal slight, and ambitious of earthly power; but in the latter, we see him patient, restful, forbearing, trustful, loving, and with the old buoyancy and courage purified and ennobled. It provides a telling illustration of the transforming power of the grace of God.

## Key words

1 The word 'precious' was evidently a favourite with Peter. Seven precious things are mentioned (1 Pet. 1: 7, 19; 2: 4, 6, 7; 3: 4; 2 Pet. 1: 1, 4).
2 Peter was radiantly buoyant; therefore it need not surprise us to find that 'hope' was another of his favourites (1: 3, 13, 21; 3: 15). While Paul has been called 'the apostle of faith', and John 'the apostle of love', Peter is called 'the apostle of hope'.
3 Peter is great on election (1: 2); foreknowledge (1: 20); Trinity (1: 2); vicarious death of Christ (1: 2, 18, 19; 2: 21, 24; 3: 18; 4: 1).
4 Peter was most teachable, and never forgot his lesson. He learned 1: 17 in Acts 10: 15, 34; 2: 4-8 in Matthew 16: 18; 2: 25 in John 10: 1; 4: 19 in Luke 23: 46; 5: 2 at John 21: 15, 17; 5: 5 in John 13: 4, 5.
5 But *the* key word is 'suffering'. This word, and its equivalent, is found twenty-one times in this short epistle, and gives the message of the book. The sufferings of Christ are referred to in every chapter, though never once in the second epistle.

---

### Able to rejoice in suffering because of
## Salvation
(1: 1-13; key 1: 6)

1 'Peter' the name Jesus gave.
2 Note the force of 'Wherein' (v.6).
3 This glorious salvation, ours through grace, enables us, through suffering and trial, 'to rejoice with joy unspeakable'.
4 And with great hope (v.13).

### That we should suffer innocently and to the glory of God
## Holiness
is essential
(1: 14 to 3: 22; key 2: 12, 19, 20; 3: 1, 17, with 4: 15, 16)

1 The imperative necessity for holiness of heart and life underlies all Peter writes in this section.
2 He is anxious that none, by careless sinful conduct, merit persecution and suffering.
3 Loose living exposes to the scorn of enemies of the cross.

### In thus suffering, we have
## Fellowship
with our Lord
(c. 4; key 4: 13)

1 Note 'they think it strange' (v.4), 'think it not strange' (v.12).
2 Provided the life is right, in suffering we are in blessed fellowship with our Lord.
3 There is a 'covering' of sin which is legitimate (v.8) — the sin of others, not our own.

### In suffering, never forget the
## Glory
which shall follow
(5: 1-4; key 5:1 with 1: 11, 13; 5: 10)

1 One blessed comfort in sorrow and trial is thought of the future.
2 This short section is full of 'the glory that should follow'.
3 'Be clothed with humility' (v.5) is literally 'Put on humility like a slave's apron'.

### Remember, suffering is
## Common
to all
(5: 5-14; key 5: 9)

1 It is not good to imagine that none suffer as we do.
2 The fact is (v.9) suffering and sorrow are experiences common to all. None are exempt.
3 'Humble yourselves' (v.6) lest he be compelled to humiliate you.

# 61
# The Second Epistle of Peter

Key word: Remembrance
Key verses: 1: 4; 2: 1, 2; 3: 17
Theme: How to be pure and loyal in days of corruption and apostasy.

## Author

There is hardly a book in the New Testament the authorship of which has been so called into question as this. Usually four objections are raised to believing that Peter wrote it, but these objections can be satisfactorily dealt with:

(a) Doubts were raised as to the Petrine authorship as far back as the third century. Answer: objections concerning other books were held in the third century, but proofs have been discovered in our own time showing how groundless these objections were.

(b) It could not have been written in Peter's lifetime, as 'all' Paul's epistles had not then been written (see 3: 16). Answer: but surely the plain sense of 3: 16 is 'all his epistles' then written!

(c) The style and language are different from that of 1 Peter. Answer: surely the fact that it was written for a different purpose settles this?

(d) Chapter 2 is evidently a copy of Jude, and surely no one dare charge the great apostle with plagiarism. Answer: neither Peter copied from Jude, nor did Jude copy from Peter. Peter, in chapter 2, prophesies (note future tense in 2: 1, 'shall be'); Jude, in vv.4, 12, 16, 17, shows that Peter's prophecy has now come to pass (note present tense 'there are').

Note — (a) the writer was an apostle (3: 2); and (b) an apostle who had been one of the privileged three on the mount of transfiguration (1: 18); (c) and had written an epistle prior to this to the same people (3: 1); (d) therefore the claim of 1: 1 is the only logical possibility.

## Contents

This letter contains a touching reference to Peter's old age and impending death (1: 14), and to his experience on the transfiguration mount (1: 17, 18). It is remarkable for its description of the Christian graces (1: 5-8), the last days (3: 4-11), and eulogy of Paul's epistles (3: 16).

## Key words

There are four words frequently met with in this epistle, and they are characteristic of the book: (a) Peter, who knew his Lord so well, speaks frequently of the value of such a knowledge of the Lord (1: 2, 3, 5, 8; 3: 18; 2: 20); (b) he was energetic, and thought highly of diligence (1: 5, 10; 3: 14); (c) he had suffered much from forgetfulness, therefore he is great on remembrance (1: 12, 13, 15; 3: 1, 2); (d) and he has much to say on corruption and pollution (1: 4; 2: 12, 19, 20).

## Purpose

This second epistle was written for a purpose altogether different from that of 1 Peter. The first was designed to encourage and support Christians under trial and persecution, but the second one was intended to warn them against false teachers and their corrupt and corrupting doctrines. This is why the Lord's sufferings are never once mentioned in the second epistle. In the first, enemies are met with; in the second, darkness is mentioned, and the need of the lamp of truth (1: 19). The first was written to console, the second to warn; in the first, we have much about suffering, in the second, much about error.

## Analysis

It falls into three divisions, as follows: (note each section has its key, cure, and safeguard.)

## Moral corruption

(1: 1-14; key 1: 4; cure — the divine name; safeguard — remembrance, 1: 12, 13)

How precious faith is obtained (v.1),
How to gain more peace and grace (v.2),
How to receive all things necessary for life and godliness (v.3),
How to escape moral corruption (v.4),
How to avoid spiritual shortsightedness (vv.5-9),
How not to fall (v.10),
How to have an abundant entrance (v.11).

## Doctrinal corruption

(1: 15 to 2: 22; key 2: 1, 2; cure — scripture, 1: 19; safeguard — remembrance, 1: 15)

Christian faith no fable (1: 16),
Divine origin of scripture (1: 17-21),
*False teachers* (2: 1),
Their large following (2: 2),
Their severe judgment (2: 3-9),
Their presumption (2: 10, 11),
Corrupt doctrine produces corrupt practices (2: 12-22).

## Steadfastness in view of corruption

(c. 3; key 3: 17; cure and safeguard — remembrance 3: 1, 2)

Even pure minds need prompting (v.1),
One fruit of false teaching is rejection of second advent truths (vv.3-9),
Certainty of the day of the Lord (v.10),
Fruit of belief in his coming is holiness of heart and life (vv.11-17).
The importance of spiritual growth (v.18).

# 62
# The First Epistle of John

Key words: Know, Fellowship
Key verses: 1: 3; 5: 18, 19, 20
Theme: The life of fellowship with God: its joyousness, victory, safety, and certainty

## Writer

This epistle, written by the aged apostle John about the year A.D. 90, probably at Ephesus, was not addressed to any particular church or individual, but to all Christians (see 2: 12-14).

## Purpose

1 Soon after the Christian church was founded, error crept into its teaching. The converts from Judaism and paganism sought to impregnate the Christian faith with their former beliefs. This led to heresy and apostasy, culminating eventually in gnosticism. This sect, while admitting the deity of Jesus, denied his humanity, and held other heretical views. They styled themselves gnostics (knowing ones), posed as 'the aristocracy of knowledge', boasted that they alone had the true knowledge, and looked down with pity and contempt upon all who were old-fashioned enough to adhere to the apostolic faith.

2 Without doubt, John had this heresy in mind when he wrote this epistle. (a) In 1: 1, 2, he declares the humanity of Christ, affirming that they had not only heard, but seen and handled him. (b) He denounces those who denied that humanity (4: 2, 3). (c) He emphasizes the fact that the gnostics had not a monopoly of knowledge; the Christian, the orthodox believer, had a knowledge derived not, as theirs, from speculation, but from revelation. (See 1: 5; 2: 20, 27.) The word 'know' and its equivalent is met with thirty-two times in this epistle. See section (4) in analysis below.

## Topical study

The topical method of study is valuable in enabling one to grasp the teaching of this letter. For instance, take three topics:

(a) LOVE: (1) God's love to sinners (4: 9, 10). (2) The outcome of that love is adoption (3: 1). (3) Why we ought to love one another (4: 11 with 3: 11, 23). (4) What the fact that we love proves (3: 14). (5) Love's absence or presence is the difference between a child of God and a child of the devil (3: 10). (6) Why we love God (4: 19). (7) What loving the world proves (2: 15). (8) In whom the love of God is matured (2: 5). (9) The result of that mature love (4: 18). (10) The greatest fact of all, that God is not only 'Light' (1: 5), but 'Love' (4: 16).

(b) SIN: (1) Its universality (1: 8, 10). (2) Two definitions of sin (3: 4; 5: 17). (3) Why our Lord came (2: 2; 3: 5; 4: 10). (4) There is cleansing from sin (1: 7) — (5) for those who confess (1: 9). (6) We may know that our sins are forgiven (2: 12). (7) No need to be continually slipping into sin (2: 1, also see 3: 8, 9). (8) Secret of overcoming sin is 'abiding' (3: 6), and 'being kept' (5: 18 RV).

(c) NEW BIRTH: Its evidence, results: (1) not continuing in sin (3: 9); (2) love (4: 7); (3) faith (5: 1); (4) Overcoming (5: 4); (5) the 'new-begotten' one is kept by the 'only-begotten' of the Father (5: 18 RV); (6) holy living (2: 29).

## Analysis: John's four reasons—

John himself gives four reasons for writing this epistle; all are the fruits of living in fellowship with God.

---

John wrote 'That your joy may be full' (1: 4). The life of fellowship is

## the joyful life

(c. 1)

1 These Christians had joy (the joy of forgiveness), but not fulness of joy (the joy of fellowship).
2 Fulness of joy is the outcome of fellowship with the Father, with Jesus Christ, and with fellow-believers.
3 This close and blessed fellowship is conditioned by —
walking in the light,
confession of sin,
forgiveness of sin,
cleansing from sin.

John wrote that they might know there was no necessity for sinning. The life of fellowship is

## the victorious life

(2: 1-17)

1 Fellowship means victory: there is no need to go on in bondage to sin, no necessity for sinning — but we do sin (v.1).
2 And for us there is an advocate through whom our fellowship can be maintained. Note that the atonement is by no means limited (vv.1, 2).
3 Fellowship with God means, and is dependent upon, obedience (vv.3-6); not loving the world (vv.15-17); loving our brethren (vv.7-11).

John wrote that they might be put on guard against error (2: 26 RV). The life of fellowship is

## the guarded life

(2: 18 to 4: 6)

1 Heresy already at work (2: 18, 19).
2 But believers were safe — guarded by the holy anointing (2: 20-27).
3 The gnostics talked a great deal, and lived badly, not so the Christians (3: 11-24).
4 Why the world hates us (3: 1).
5 The marks of false teachers (4: 1-6).

John wrote 'That ye may know' (5: 13). The life of fellowship is

## the life of knowledge

(4: 7 to 5: 21)

1 A knowledge that rests upon the testimony of God's Word and God's Spirit (5: 6-12).
2 For what we know, consider the following passages:
2: 3, 5, 13, 14, 20, 21, 29.
3: 2, 5, 14, 15, 19, 24.
4: 2, 6, 13, 16.
5: 2, 13, 15, 18, 19, 20.

# 63
# The Second Epistle of John

Key word: Truth
Key verse: v.2
Theme: Truth must be received, obeyed, and cherished at all costs

## Nature

1 This epistle is notable as being the only one in the New Testament exclusively addressed to a lady.
2 It is a private, personal letter, addressed to an unknown Christian woman and her family, and is a charming example of the private correspondence of the apostles, and of the early Christian church.
3 Who the 'lady' was is not known. Some consider that the words 'elect lady' constitute a title, proving that the individual was one who was well-to-do, and moved in high society. There is a tradition that the person addressed was Martha of Bethany. Bengel says that the Greek 'kyria' (lady) answers to the Hebrew 'Martha'. If this be true, the 'sister' referred to in verse 13 would be Mary.

## Author

1 Owing to the absence of a name in the introduction, the authorship of this epistle has been much disputed.
2 There is every evidence that John wrote it. It resembles his first epistle very closely — eight of its thirteen verses may be found in the first epistle, either in sense or expression. John must have been a very old man when he wrote it — he calls himself 'Elder' — at least ninety years of age.

## Purpose

1 The word 'love' occurs four times in this short epistle (vv.1, 3, 5, 6), 'truth' five times (vv.1, 2, 3, 4).
2 It appears to have been written to warn a benevolent lady against entertaining some false teachers (v.10).

## Key

1 Without doubt, truth must be considered the key-wo this epistle, and as providing its message.
2 That word is used in three senses: (1) for the body Christian teaching (vv.1, 4); (2) for Christ himself; (3) 'truly'.
3 Thus it provides us with a little homily on truth, giving us its nature, test, fruit, character, and defence.

---

## Love in the truth
(v.1)

1 John did not scruple to give this lady her own title of honour.
2 Truth as the:
(a) Source of love (see RV).
(b) Nature of love (no pretence of love).
(c) Reason for love (her loyalty to truth).
3 Not only John, but all who knew her and her family, loved them.

## For sake of the truth
(v.2)

1 Can we not spell Truth here with a capital 'T'? He is Truth.
2 He, as Truth, is: within us, with us, and for his sake we love and do.

## Salutation in the truth
(v.3)

1 A most unusual form of salutation, found elsewhere only in the Pastoral epistles.
2 We need grace, mercy, and peace.
3 Note the combination of divine names.

## Walking in the truth
(vv.4-6)

1 'Certain of' is RV of v.4.
2 Truth is given to walk in (v.4).
3 We must love (v.5).
4 And love manifests itself in ready obedience (v.6).

## The test of the truth
(vv.7-9)

1 Denying the reality of Christ's humanity,
(a) In his earthly life,
(b) and in his second advent (see RV) is one mark of antichrist and of false teachers.
2 Don't be crownless (v.8).

## Defence of the truth
(vv.10-13)

1 There is a false charity.
2 In defence of the truth, we must not entertain, or bid god-speed, to false teachers.
3 An affectionate ending (vv.12, 13).

# 64
# The Third Epistle of John

**Key word: Fellow-helpers**
**Key verse: v.8**
**Themes: (1) The duty of hospitality in the church**
**(2) The peril of domineering leadership**

**For whom**
1 This letter was written 'unto the well-beloved Gaius' (v.1), by the apostle John when an aged man.
2 There are five individuals referred to by this name:

(1) Gaius of Macedonia (Acts 19: 29); (2) Gaius of Derbe (Acts 20: 4); (3) one whom Paul baptised (1 Cor. 1: 14); (4) one of Paul's hosts (Rom, 16: 23); (5) and the one John wrote to. Probably the last three were one and the same.
3 Therefore we learn that Gaius was converted through John (v.4), baptised by Paul, and was a wealthy and hospitable member of the church at Corinth.

**Purpose**
1 Many of the early Christians were called to a life of itinerant evangelism, without fee or earthly reward (v.7); consequently they were dependent upon the hospitality of the Christians settled in the various towns, villages, or cities they passed through.
2 A man called Diotrephes had secured almost absolute control over this church, and in a domineering and autocratic manner refused to entertain or allow these evangelists to minister there, and excommunicated the hospitable church members who did receive them (v.10). John had written to the church about the matter (one of the many lost epistles), but Diotrephes had rejected it, and would not acknowledge John's apostolic authority (v.9).
3 The aged apostle now wrote to generous and warm-hearted Gaius, commending him for past kindnesses shown, and urging him to continue his most God-like work of entertaining the Lord's servants in spite of Diotrephes (vv.5,

6, 8), promising to deal drastically with this usurper when he next visited that church (v.10).

**Contrast**
A striking contrast is seen in the three persons mentioned in this short epistle: (1) Gaius, the kind, generous, and hospitable; (2) Diotrephes, the arrogant church official; and (3) Demetrius, who was praised by all.

**Contribution**
Though this letter contains no important doctrinal teaching, it is yet of great value, as showing the beginning of arrogant, autocratic, and domineering leadership, which has been such a curse to the Christian church, in the past, as in the present. Even an apostle's authority was called into question.

**Truth**
As in the second epistle, the word 'truth' is frequently referred to. Truth is viewed: (1) as the source and nature of the apostle's love (v.1); (2) as an inward presence and power (v.3); (3) manifesting itself in outward practice (vv.3, 4). We are exhorted to use truth as our weapon in Christian service and warfare — (see v.8 RV), and as our companion and partner (v.8 AV/KJV). Truth will then give its testimony in our favour (v.12).

---

## INTRODUCTION, SALUTATION

**The apostle's**
### Love
**(v.1)**
1 Note the strong affection of the apostle.
2 His love was sincere (RV), rooted in truth. On account of the truth.

**The apostle's**
### Prayer
**(v.2)**
1 Not merely a wish, but, as RV shows, a prayer.
2 Was Gaius ill and weak in body?
3 He was well in soul.
4 Look well at RV.

**The apostle's**
### Rejoicing
**(vv.3, 4)**
1 Truth was to Gaius an indwelling power, a road he walked on, an atmosphere he breathed.
2 Note what John rejoiced over.

## THE PURPOSE

**The apostle's**
**commendation and**
### Exhortation
**(vv.5-8)**
1 By 'brethren and strangers', John means converted Jews and Gentiles.
2 One can hardly tell where commendation ends and exhortation begins.
3 Read vv.7, 8 in RV.

**The apostle's**
### Denunciation
**(vv.9-11)**
1 This letter is lost.
2 Diotrephes —
loved to be in front,
rejected John's letter,
backbit John,
was inhospitable,
commended inhospitality,
cast out the hospitable.

## CONCLUSION

**The apostle's**
### Commendation
**(v.12)**
1 Was this the Demetrius of Acts 19: 24? If so, what a change!
2 He had good opinion
of all men,
of truth itself,
of the apostle,
of other Christians.

**The apostle's**
### Explanation
**(vv.13, 14)**
1 John explains why he wrote so brief a letter.
2 The apostle valued friendship.

# 65
# The Epistle of Jude

**Key words: Keep, kept**
**Key verses: vv.1, 6, 21, 24**
**Theme: Our duty, in view of apostasy, is to keep the faith, and trust to be kept from stumbling.**

**Author**
1 Jude, (another form of Judas), brother to our Lord and to James (Matt. 13: 55; Mark 6: 3), was the author of this letter.
2 Like James, he was not an apostle, but an ordinary disciple. 'He was a plain man, but of fiery spirit, and filled with prophetic zeal'; yet, behind all that austerity beat a warm and loving heart — note occurrence of the term, 'beloved' (vv.3, 17, 20).

**To whom?**
1 It must have been written about A.D. 69, as he refers to the prophecy in 2 Peter, and that was not written until A.D. 66. His brother James had died a martyr a few years before he wrote this letter.
2 It was not written to any particular church or people, but to all Christians everywhere, hence called a 'General Epistle'.

**Why written**
1 From v.3 it appears he was about to write a treatise on salvation, when he was constrained by the Spirit to change its theme. Already the primitive church was in dire peril through traitors within it, through many who had deliberately rejected the faith, though still retaining their membership. He writes to warn them, and to put them on their guard.

2 Jude's epistle is one of the most solemn in the Bible. It gives a history of apostasy from before time to the end of time, dealing with the ambitious angels, self-righteous Cain, depraved Sodomites, rebellious Israel, greedy Balaam, presumptuous Korah, and the apostasy of his own day and ours; in all, three judgments on corporate wickedness, and three on individual.

**Notes**
1 It is the only book in the Bible which records the strife over the body of Moses (v.9), and Enoch's prophecy (vv.14, 15).
2 Three eternal things are mentioned: (1) life (v.21); (2) chains (v.6); (5) fire (v.7).
3 Its key words are 'keep' and 'kept', mentioned five times (vv.1, 6 RV; 21, 24 AV/KJV).

---

To whom written?
To the Lord's people who were

## kept by God for the Lord Jesus
**(vv.1, 2)**
1 RV for 'preserved' is 'kept for Jesus Christ'.
2 It is written to those who are (as RV) —
called ones,
beloved of God,
preserved through union with Christ,
and 'kept for Jesus Christ', as a precious gift to be presented to him by God, the father.

Why was it written?
To exhort the Lord's people to contend for and to

## keep the faith
**(vv.3, 4)**
1 Note v.3 RV: the Holy Spirit constrained him to change his theme.
2 'Common' salvation does not mean salvation that is of little value, but salvation available for all.
3 'Once delivered' means needing no further commendation; incapable of improvement.

Past instances of apostasy: those who did not keep to paths of truth and obedience are

## kept unto judgment
**(vv.5-7)**
1 As a warning, they are reminded of well-known instances of apostasy, upon whom the severe judgment of God fell in this life, with the certainty of judgment in the future.
2 Those who 'kept not' are 'kept' (RV) — reserved unto judgment.

Vivid description of the character of the apostates — their disastrous deterioration of character through

## not keeping the faith
**(vv.8-19)**
To forsake the faith leads to terrible deterioration in character:
Loose morals (vv.19, 18),
Corrupt thoughts (vv.8, 10),
Impatience of control (vv.8, 16),
Mocking spirit (vv.8, 18),
Boastful words (vv.8, 10, 16),
Sham-religion (vv.12, 13, 19),
'Hidden rocks' (a danger to others) (v.12 RV).
Always complaining (v.16).
Weymouth's version has, 'These men are murmurers, complaining of their lot'.

Necessity of keeping in love, as well as in the faith: the Lord's people to see that they are

## kept in the love of God
**(vv.20-23)**
1 It is possible to be loyal to truth yet lack love.
2 Note, there must be on our part: building (v.20), praying (v.20), keeping (v.21), looking (v.21), pitying (v.22), saving (v.23), hating (v.23).

A remarkable and beautiful doxology: the Lord's people to be

## kept from stumbling
**(vv.24, 25)**
1 How glorious, that he is able to keep us from even 'stumbling' (RV), let alone 'falling'.

# 66
# The Book of the Revelation

Key phrase: 'The Revelation of Jesus Christ'
Key verse: 1: 19
Theme: Jesus, the gloriously triumphant one

## Difficult book

This is confessedly the book of the Bible most difficult of interpretation; and because of this, though a special blessing is promised to its readers (1: 3), it is very much neglected. We cannot but think that Satan has something to do with this neglect, because it has so much to say about his final downfall. Why should we pass the book by just because it is mysterious and difficult? Do men of science leave scientific problems alone because they happen to be difficult to comprehend?

## Splendid finish to Bible

It makes a splendid finish to the divine library. Archibald G. Brown points out the striking balance between Genesis and Revelation. 'In Genesis I see earth created; in Revelation I see it passing away. In Genesis sun and moon appear; in Revelation, they have no need of sun or moon. In Genesis there is a garden, the home for man; in Revelation, a city, the home for the nations. In Genesis there is the marriage of the first Adam; in Revelation, the marriage of the second Adam. In Genesis there is the first grim appearance of that great enemy Satan; in Revelation, his final doom. In Genesis there is the inauguration of sorrow and suffering, the first sob, the first tear; in Revelation, no more sorrow, no more pain, and all tears are wiped away. In Genesis we hear the mutter of the curse, which falls because of sin; in Revelation we read there shall be no more curse. In Genesis we see man driven out from the garden with the tree of life; in Revelation we see him welcomed back, with the tree of life at his disposal.'

## Clues

In order to right understanding of the book, several facts must be constantly kept in mind:
1 It gives a glowing portrait of the Lord Jesus as the triumphant one. The key phrase is 'the revelation of Jesus Christ'. It unveils the Lord Jesus. 'Whoever sets upon the study of the book to find out what it says about the Lord Jesus, will find it a marvellous revelation.' No less than twenty-six times do we find in it Christ's sacrificial title 'Lamb'. It is full of him.
2 After the end of c. 3 the church is never represented as on the earth in this book. Between cc. 3 and 4 the removal of the church must have taken place; c. 4 and onward has to do with the awful tribulation and last things.
3 The law of recurrence (to be observed in other books of the Bible) must be noted. After reviewing some great procession or national event, we usually give an account to our loved ones of what we have seen, returning to the subject again and again to give additional particulars. This is 'recurrence', and precisely what John does. After giving an account of the beginning of the judgments on the earth, and the final victory of the Lord Jesus (4: 1 to 11: 18 see analysis below), he returns to the subject in 11: 19 to 16: 21, and again in cc. 17 to 22. It is most important to keep this law of recurrence in mind when reading Revelation.

## Analysis

1: 19 gives the three-fold division, the last section falling into three sub-sections.

## 'The things which thou hast seen'

### The Lord Jesus as the glorified one

(c. 1)
1 'Revelation', not revelations.
2 Of Jesus, and not of John.
3 Blessing for readers and hearers (v.3).
4 Glowing vision of the Lord Jesus.
5 Observe v.5 RV 'loveth' (present tense) — he still loves.

## 'The things which are'

### The Lord Jesus as the head over the church

(cc. 2, 3)
1 The Lord's striking message to the seven churches of Asia, still applicable to the churches of today.
2 Before the vision of the father in 4: 3, the vision and words of the son in cc. 1 to 3; we must get to know the son before we can savingly know the father — he is the way to God.

## 'The things which shall be hereafter'

### The Lord Jesus as the triumphant one

**(1) (4: 1 to 11: 18)**
1 Scene shifts to heaven, audience chamber of the Most High.
2 The book, c. 5, is not that of life, but of judgment.
3 The tribulation begins with the opening of the seals (c. 6).
4 The plagues increase in severity in succeeding chapters.
5 C. 7 must be considered a parenthesis, a welcome view of the Lord preserving his own.
6 At last, the final, complete victory of our divine and ever-blessed Lord.

**(2) (11: 19 to 16: 21)**
1 The former division had to do with secular evil, its standpoint the Throne; this division has to do with spiritual wickedness, its standpoint the Temple.
2 In former divisions we began with Christ the glorified one; here we are taken further back, to his birth and the devil's attempts to get rid of him.
3 The rise and progress of the awful trinity of evil.
4 Then a sight of Christ as conqueror, defeat of the allied forces of evil, and fall of Babylon.

**(3) (cc. 17 to 22)**
1 We are again introduced to the last things, to get particulars about —
Fall of Babylon (cc. 17, 18);
Advent of Christ the conqueror, and marriage of the Lamb (c. 19);
Satan's fall, imprisonment, final overthrow and end (c. 20); new heavens and earth (c. 21); Garden City, last words of Jesus (c. 22).
2 Note, four woes and four alleluias in c. 19:— nine references to woe, yet ten songs.